When God walked on campus

When God walked on campus

A brief history of evangelical awakenings at American colleges and universities

Michael F. Gleason

press

Dundas, Ontario

Other titles by Michael F. Gleason

Building on Living Stones: New Testament Patterns and Principles of Renewal

Now to him who is able to do immeasurably more than all we ask or imagine, according to his power that is at work within us, to him be glory in the church and in Christ Jesus throughout all generations, for ever and ever! Amen.
—*Ephesians 3:20–21*, NIV

Joshua Press Inc., Dundas, Ontario, Canada
Fax 905.627.8451 www.joshuapress.com

Editorial director: Michael A.G. Haykin
Creative/production manager: Janice Van Eck

© Cover photo by Paul Weeks
© Cover & book design by Janice Van Eck

Our special thanks to Crossway Books, a division of Good News Publishers, Wheaton, Illinois 60187 for permission to reprint chapter 24, "Revival: The presence of God's Spirit among us" from *Revival*, by Martyn Lloyd-Jones, © 1987.

National Library of Canada Cataloguing in Publication Data

Gleason, Michael, 1953–
    When God walked on campus: a brief history of evangelical awakenings at American colleges and universities

Includes bibliographical references.
ISBN 1-894400-16-X

1. Universities and colleges—United States—Religion—History. 2. Revivals—United States—History. 3. Evangelistic work—United States—History. I. Title.

| BV1610.G44 2002 | 269'.24'0973 | C2001-904307-4 |
| F674.A44B68 2002 | 978.2'94 | C2001-904312-0 |

Dedicated to all students, and especially those at Ashland University

Contents

Foreword

Michael and I met when he was invited to attend the North American Convocation on Revival that I co-hosted in Little Rock, Arkansas, in February 1995. There, among some of North America's most prominent Christian leaders, Michael stood out to me as a man who had an authentic passion for revival. Later, when he asked me to visit Ashland University, Michael began showing me the mountain of information he was collecting: source material, first-hand accounts, thrilling written recollections of days when God came to the campuses. He did not just want to talk about revival, but longed to see God "rend the heavens and come down" just as he had done in the past. We prayed, talked and have since corresponded about just that.

The author has been careful to be accurate and not to bring his own agenda to the book. He has correctly delineated between experience- and Word-driven revivals, for instance, indicating the deficiencies of the former. The college revivals have principally been experience-driven revivals, as he makes clear, but true revivals nonetheless. I am appreciative for this clarity. If we are going to ask for revival, let us ask for the kind that will be the most long-lasting and most pleasing to God.

Adding the messages of Timothy Dwight, Charles Spurgeon, Martin Lloyd-Jones and J. Edwin Orr has added a useful dimension for reflection, although Gleason's popular but accurate survey stands sufficiently by itself. Michael Haykin's short life of Orr is an important extra for those of us who recognize Orr's place in revival studies.

Because the history of past revivals has often been the means of creating a burden for revival in the present, I am optimistic about this small book. Revival literature is addictive in that it speaks of hope. The worst of situations can become, with God's presence, the most God-honouring and beautiful. God may well come to the campuses again, a favoured place for the Holy Spirit's work in the past. Let's use this book to motivate us to prayer, as a resource for teaching, as a study for campus ministry meetings, for the training of leaders, for preparing college-bound students, for equipping ministers in our seminaries and to cause us all to hope again.

Jim Elliff
Christian Communicators Worldwide
Kansas City, Missouri

Acknowledgements

Nearly every work is the product of many lives and such is the case with this small volume. Those who assisted in its completion are numerous, but in particular I would like to express my appreciation to Eric Bargerhuff, Jim Elliff, Mack Tomlinson, Dr. R. Albert Mohler, Jr., Richard Owen Roberts, Joseph Maggelet, Dr. Michael Haykin and the fine staff of Joshua Press for their thoughtful encouragement and pertinent editorial advice. Finally, I would be amiss to not extend gratitude to my parents, Charles and Nancy Gleason, under whose guidance I was first exposed to the Christian church.

1

An invitation to begin

Be forewarned! The book you are about to read may well create a deep and abiding spiritual yearning, as throughout the following chapters you witness the phenomenal transformation that occurred within student lives when God walked on campus. Do you need an illustration? When God walked on the Princeton campus in 1815 we are told that his presence "seemed to descend like the silent dew of heaven; and in about four weeks, there were very few individuals in the College edifice who were not deeply impressed with a sense of the importance of spiritual and eternal things. There was scarcely a room—perhaps not one—which was not a place of earnest secret devotion."[1] A similar occurrence was noted around 1858 at Amherst College in Massachusetts when, as a result of God's visitation to the campus in power, President William A. Stearns reported that "of the Senior Class, but three or four remain who have not openly commenced the Christian Life. Of the Junior Class, but one, and he is a serious inquirer, if not a Christian. Of the Sophomore Class, four or five. Of the Freshman Class, nine or ten."[2]

Do you think such occurrences in this day are impossible? In human terms, they are! What we're talking about, however, is revival. In its purest form, revival is nothing short of God impacting human history in an extraordinary or phenomenal way. It is what one encounters in reading the book of Acts. Men like Peter, without a formal education (see Acts 4:13), being used by God to win thousands to the Saviour. That's revival!

When God visited various American campuses throughout the past two centuries, it was often the "untrained" student leaders, such as Peter Parker, a senior at Yale in 1831, who played a significant role in the harvesting of student souls. The divine visitation that graced his campus during that year yielded seventy-four hearts committed to Christ, nearly one quarter of the entire campus.[3] When God walks on campus anew in the coming great awakening, who will it be that he might call to work in the bountiful fields of harvest—perhaps you?

Is your interest growing? If so, go back in time with me to the first great revival of the Christian era: Acts 1. We have a lot in common with those first-century Christians. Their society was often skeptical towards the Christian message, like so many university campuses today. Their Master had given them the command to "be my witnesses in Jerusalem, and in all Judea and Samaria, and to the ends of the earth" (Acts 1:8), a command that was literally impossible to fulfill, considering their resources and collective abilities. Sound familiar? How do *you* respond when confronted with an impossible challenge, such as the hopeful event of God walking on your campus and causing every dorm room to be "a place of earnest secret devotion?" Pause for a moment and allow your mind to imagine what that experience might be like.

The early Christians practiced only one initial strategy in response to their Master's charge. They gathered with a small group of disciples in an upper room for earnest and dependent intercession (Acts 1:14). Conceivably, some of them may well have thought: "Lord, what you are asking for can only occur if you come in great power, for we have neither the resources nor the abilities to reach our entire world. Apart from the outpouring of your Spirit, it just will not be!"

Now, I am certainly not suggesting that the Christian community should shelter itself in perpetual prayer meetings while the disciplines of solid Scripture study and outreach remain neglected. But is it through these disciplines *alone* that the majority of the students on your campus will be reached? Are the best of your obedient efforts and structured programs, important as they may be, going to cultivate the harvest of souls that Princeton enjoyed in 1815, Yale in 1831 and Amherst in 1858? Your yearning for God to again walk on campus in an extraordinary or phenomenal way is perhaps similar to mine. If that is indeed your desire, then your heart seeks nothing short of revival.

I do believe, however, that a word of caution should be offered at this point that may be especially applicable to a college audience. A study of the history of recent revivals reveals a recurrent tendency within the Christian community to pursue the "experiences" and "blessings" of revival, rather than its Author and his most holy decrees. The unfortunate and common fruit of this imbalance are revivals deficient in both duration and effect. Revival historian Richard Owen Roberts suggests the following insights concerning this observation:

> As a generalization, revivals fall into two distinct categories: experience-centered and Word-centered. Experience-centered revivals, of which the Welsh revival of 1904–1905 and the Jesus people revival of 1971–1972[4] are good examples, tend to last briefly, end abruptly, and result in only minor reforms, if any. Word-centered revivals may be expected to endure a long time, possibly even an entire generation, to restore to the church certain great biblical truths that have been neglected, and are almost guaranteed to produce long-range moral and social improvements. Both the sixteenth-century Protestant Reformation and the eighteenth-century Evangelical Revival/Great Awakening are primary examples of this second kind of revival. Confession, prayer and praise are the prominent activities in an experience-centered revival. Spirit-anointed preaching producing profound conviction, glorious resuscitation of individuals and churches, and radical conversions are the expected norm of the Word-centered revival.[5]

The following chart will help to clarify the important characteristics of each term as thoughtfully articulated by Roberts:

Word-centred revivals	Experience-centred revivals
In-depth Spirit-anointed preaching and teaching are central in large and small group meetings that produce confession, prayer and praise. Such teaching is aimed at the restoration of the Christian community to the great biblical truths that have been long neglected: • the majestic attributes of God, Christ and the Holy Spirit • justification by faith alone • the characteristics of genuine repentance and authentic conversion • disciplined prayer • practicing the faith through service, evangelism and missions	Confession, prayer and praise are central elements in large and small group meetings. Teaching at such gatherings frequently lacks depth and substance.
Conversions are numerous, and are often nurtured through biblically based small groups.	Conversions are numerous, with tragically little follow-up.
The seeking of God becomes central.	Often the seeking of revival "experiences" becomes the goal of the participant.
Historically, they endure a long time, restore the church to certain great biblical truths and produce long-range moral and social improvements. The First Great Awakening is an excellent example of a Word-centred revival.	Historically, they last briefly, end abruptly and are comparatively devoid of long-term reformation. Such was the case with the Welsh revival of 1904, the Jesus people revival in 1971 and the minor collegiate revival of 1995.

Compare and contrast again the various descriptions with the adjacent summary. Whereas the "seeking of God" is central within the Word-centred movements, the seeking of "revival experiences" is often the focus of experience-centred gatherings. Profound, protracted and in-depth biblical teaching are central within Word-centred movements, as illustrated throughout the various sermons catalogued at the conclusion of the next four chapters. The reader is encouraged to read these texts, and observe how scripturally soaked and God-honouring they are. On the other hand, as the experience-centred movements are studied one becomes aware of the fact that the leaders may tend to champion messages that are notably deficient in both depth and substance. Indeed, one might say that a Word-centred revival produces not only the confession, prayer and praise common to experience-centred movements, but also long-term reformation with regard to both doctrine and practice.

My research has led me to conclude, sadly, that the student awakenings, particularly within recent decades, have been frequently experience-centred and thus brief in scope and comparatively deficient in producing the long-term purification common to Word-centred movements. It is likewise my current concern that the general superficiality of our prevailing Christian culture may well prompt the believing community to look no further than for another short-lived "blessing," when the average university campus is in deep need of sustained spiritual, moral and social renovation.

If, however, it is indeed a Word-centred revival that *you* seek, then both the content and format of this book may be of particular help to you. At the conclusion of each of the successive chapters you will be furnished with several challenging questions for individual or group reflection. The general goal of these questions is to assist each reader in wrestling with issues such as personal and corporate repentance, faith, obedience, intercession, evangelism and the like which are common concerns in both experience- and Word-centred visitations. The final question in each series is, however, somewhat unique. This question will provide a challenge to sit under the preaching of four outstanding Christian leaders whose voices throughout the centuries inspired a yearning for revival in the hearts of untold lives. As you study these messages you will come to know one of the first presidents of Yale College whose administration witnessed no less than four student revivals— Timothy Dwight (1752–1817); a gifted nineteenth-century preacher whose life often impacted students and whose heart continually burned for revival—Charles Haddon Spurgeon (1834–1892); the president of Europe's 1939 InterVarsity Fellowship and a man thought by many to be the greatest preacher of the past century— D. Martyn Lloyd-Jones (1899–1981); and finally a gifted scholar, writer and evangelist used of God to promote revival throughout various seasons of student awakenings—J. Edwin Orr (1912–1987). Listen to these great leaders speak, and contrast the depth of their teaching to what you currently are experiencing in your church or student fellowship. Read of the conditions prevalent within the nations and respective communities in which these doctrinally rich messages were first proclaimed. Generally speaking, the messages were preached during difficult times, and yet these leaders brought their drifting culture and wayward audience to God through passionate in-depth biblical teaching. Oh that the sacred Scripture might again be preached in its fullness within the wider Christian community! Oh that God might again raise up such voices, such conviction, such burden, such teachers of the Word!

Are you ready to begin your journey through two centuries of collegiate revival history? If so, might I encourage each traveller with one additional thought? As you commence this pilgrimage, know that both my prayers, along with those of countless others, are being sent heavenward on your behalf. You are part of a strong and growing movement of university students who yearn to again see the footprints of God on their campus, and what better way to honour our esteemed Guest than to prepare our hearts for his coming. Shall we begin?

For reflection [6]

Read and meditate on Acts 1–2 and then answer the following questions:

1. Acts 1:4–5: What do these verses say about the Holy Spirit with regard to ministry? Notice that this passage is a parallel to the words of Christ in Luke 24:49.

2. Acts 1:6: What did the early disciples still think Jesus was going to do?

3. Acts 1:7–8: What is to be the central task of the believing community according to these words of Jesus?

4. Acts 1:8: "Power" in the original Greek is *dynamis*. Our English word "dynamite" is derived from this Greek term. What does the use of this term say about the impact of the Holy Spirit within the lives of believers?

5. Acts 1:8: "Jerusalem, and in all Judea and Samaria, and to the ends of the earth." Observe how Jesus gave them an "impossible" task! How could they fulfill this command?

6. Acts 1:14: What is the relationship between this verse and the "impossible" task of Acts 1:8?

7. Acts 2:1–12: Why were the "tongues of fire" given?

8. Acts 2:14–41: Although, as is noted in 2:40, the entire message of Peter is not included in this portion of Acts, take a moment to cross-reference this segment of his address to the numerous corresponding Old Testament texts upon which it was built. Was Peter's sermon in Acts 2 Word-centred? Why or why not? Was it also Christ-centred? Why or why not?

9. Acts 2:37–41: What was the fruit of his sermon?

10. Acts 2:42–47: What four elements appear to have been central in the first Christian community?

Covenant

Now comes the binding labour! Using insights gained from Acts 1–2, combined with your own personal thoughts, complete the statement of prayer below. This statement should reflect what you yearn for the Holy Spirit to accomplish both in and through you. Some, for example, may be convicted with a desire to be known as a "witness" for Christ, in the fullest sense of the term, embracing a total and complete surrender to the Lord in every area of life. Others may have been impressed to practice disciplined prayer for a revival on their campus that is so vast in scope and power that nothing less than the dynamis, or power of the Holy Spirit, could cause it to come to pass. Perhaps some may be touched to deepen their commitments to personal Scripture study, a stronger Word-centred teaching ministry, the Christian community or various forms of outreach. Challenges at the conclusion of upcoming studies will provide additional opportunities for you to refine or add to your original statement of prayer petitions.

Statement of prayer

It is my prayer that the Holy Spirit will help me...

1   Joshua Bradley, *Accounts of Religious Revivals in Many Parts of The United States from 1815–1818* (Wheaton, Illinois: Richard Owen Roberts Publishers, 1980), 252–253.

2   *The Oberlin Evangelist* (May 12, 1858).

3   H.B. Wright, *Two Centuries of Christian Activity at Yale* (New York: G.P. Putnam's Sons, 1901), passim.

4   I would also suggest that the visitation of God on various Amerian college campuses in the spring of 1995 be characterized as an experience-centred revival. See pp.104–106.

5   Richard Owen Roberts, *Whitefield In Print* (Wheaton, Illinois: Richard Owen Roberts Publishers, 1988), xii.

6   These questions were adapted from the author's *Building on Living Stones: New Testament Patterns and Principles of Renewal* (Grand Rapids, Michigan: Kregel Publications, 1996).

2

"Like the silent dew of heaven"

Campus revivals in the early nineteenth century

The setting

Some view the early settlers of nineteenth-century America as basically fine, upstanding citizens; in other words, they were moral men and women with little need of spiritual revival. In similar fashion, others may picture the typical university campus of that time period as predominately a pious, church-related institution, with saintly young men and women seeking to enrich both their mind and soul at the feet of godly instructors. True? Well, yes, at times. The early colleges were primarily church-related. Godly instructors and saintly students? That depends on the school, the era, the administration, the student leaders and, most notably, the divine administration of grace.

Visit, for example, Yale College at the turn of the eighteenth century. Even under the capable leadership of President Timothy Dwight,[1] the students were influenced by a culture steeped in values that reflected little biblical bias. In that age, the impact of the French Revolution upon western society had led to a corruption of both culture and mind, the long-term fruit of which was evidenced in the lives of the upcoming generation. Lyman Beecher (1775–1863), a student at Yale at the turn of the century, described the college in this way:

> Before he [Timothy Dwight] came, the college was in a most ungodly state. The college church was almost extinct. Most

of the students were skeptical, and rowdies were plenty. Wine and liquors were kept in many rooms; intemperance, profanity, gambling, and licentiousness were common. I hardly know how I escaped....That was the day of the infidelity of the Tom Paine school. Boys that dressed flax in the barn, as I used to, read Tom Paine and believed him; I read, and fought him all the way. Never had any propensity to infidelity. But most of the class before me were infidels, and called each other Voltaire, Rousseau, D'Alembert, etc.[2]

Princeton College, like Yale, had its share of rowdies. In February 1780, for example, approximately half the student body participated in what was called a "serious riot" to protest a decision by the administration to suspend several pupils for an offense most considered to be "minor." Pistols were fired, dormitory walls and doors defaced, and general chaos prevailed. Only when the president threatened to "shut up the college till the board of trustees met" did the disorder cease.[3] In the middle of the next decade several students broke into the Prayer Hall at Princeton with the goal of cutting through the pages of the pulpit Bible so that a deck of playing cards could be inserted. They succeeded. This act of desecration was followed by a more outwardly destructive incident on the night of January 9, 1814, when two pounds of gunpowder were packed in a log and ignited inside Nassau Hall, blowing out windows and cracking walls from foundation to ceiling.[4]

Harvard was also plagued with the influence of what S.E. Morison called "French Mania." He describes the typical student at the close of the eighteenth century as "an atheist in religion, an experimentalist in morals, a rebel to authority."[5] Theology followed morals when, in 1805, Harvard elected to the divinity professorship an avowed Unitarian by the name of Henry Ware (1764–1845).[6]

Another Massachusetts institution, Williams College, is reported to have graduated only five professing Christians during the first seven years of its existence, with mockery and insult heaped upon students who showed signs of turning toward the faith.[7] An alumnus of one of the early classes of Williams reported: "Everybody at that day drank…it excited the animal spirits, it mattered not much what the liquor was. Some kept this in their rooms, and indulged in its use in their convivial meetings without concealment or disgrace."[8]

Three devout students at Brown University formed a "College Praying Society" that met weekly "in a private room, secretly, for fear of disturbance from the unpentitent."[9] Over a decade later, in a letter to fellow believers at Williams College, a despairing student remarked: "We did hope that God would open the windows of heaven upon this thirsty spot; but He is pleased to pass by at such a distance, that we feel but little of His influence."[10]

At Hampden-Sydney College, located in Cumberland County, Virginia, three young hearts were awakened to belief around the turn of the century and started meeting quietly in their room for songs, prayer and Scripture reading. Their fellow students would gather as a mob outside the dorm room and, with swearing, ridicule and threats, demand that the prayer meetings cease.[11]

It is no surprise to discover that Bowdoin College was also void of genuine spirituality, for it was situated in a small Maine community by the name of Brunswick, which in this era emulated much that was shameful and opposed to the Christian faith. A brief description of the College and surrounding community, as viewed through the eyes of Bowdoin College's Professor Smyth, will illustrate: "In several parishes in this vicinity the ministers were notoriously intemperate. Rum flowed down the streets. Sabbath breaking and profaneness were greatly prevalent….Moral restraints generally were deplorably relaxed."[12]

An article in the 1859 *Princeton Review* reported Professor Smyth's reflective remarks of his early years at Bowdoin College with the following summary: "During the first four years of Dr. McKeen's administration (1802–1806), though some of the students were thoughtful, upright, and possessed of fine intellectual abilities and social qualities, there was not one, it is believed, who was a member of any church, or believed and hoped in Christ as his

Saviour!"[13] The majority of Professor Smyth's associates at Bowdoin echoed his sentiments as they reported to their colleagues elsewhere, "We assure you this is a most wretched place."[14]

Writing on the general conditions of early American college life, Fred W. Hoffman suggests that "the colleges of the land were seedbeds of infidelity. The teachings of Deism, with its rejection of Christianity, were almost universally adopted."[15] There are numerous other examples of what we have already seen. For instance, Transylvania College in Kentucky, which had been founded by Presbyterians, came under the control of those whose beliefs differed greatly from the orthodox faith of their founders. There were others, who with an increasingly rationalistic world view, were teaching in the University of Pennsylvania and in Columbia College, South Carolina.

Dartmouth College, sorrowfully, was also not able to withstand the national onslaught of spiritual betrayal. Only one solitary member of the class of 1799 at Dartmouth was known by his peers as a professing Christian.[16] Some words of Joel Parker, who pastored at West Hartford, Connecticut, provide perhaps the best synopsis: "It seemed as if God had almost entirely withdrawn His gracious influence. We were left to mourn an absent God, barren ordinances, unsuccessful Gospel and cold hearts."[17]

How can God move in such times? Voltaire (1694–1778), one of the leading representatives of French rationalist thought, brazenly declared that God's eternal Word would, within thirty years, pass into "the limbo of forgotten literature."[18] Foundations were crumbling, the believing community appeared to be wasting away and God appeared to be silent. Can God move in such times as these, such times as ours, for our day bears a striking resemblance to that era? Read on!

The awakening and expansion

God has a penchant for creating order out of chaos. The first work he ever displayed in creation, as we know it, was to bring into being a planet that was "formless and empty" (Genesis 1:2). In the midst of chaos he created tremendous order and bounty. He spoke, and the measureless power of God caused it to be. When God commands a formless and empty planet to be both shaped and filled, even the rocks and stones obey!

So it is with spiritual awakening. When, for example, the God of creation chose to walk among the academic halls and wooded grounds of Yale College in 1802, a spiritual revival occurred that "shook the institution to its center."[19] According to Lyman Beecher, then a student there and quoted earlier in this chapter, the presence of God was so great that "all infidelity sulked and hid its head."[20] A young tutor by the name of Benjamin Silliman was converted at the time of the revival and shared the following perspective of this work of God in a letter to his mother: "Yale College is a little temple: prayer and praise seem to be the delight of the greater part of the students while those who are still unfeeling are awed into respectful silence."[21] To the joy of Timothy Dwight, out of the 230 students then in college, about one-third were powerfully converted with nearly half the new believers ultimately responding positively to a call to vocational ministry.[22] And all this occurred in a period of less than six months!

God, however, did not limit his acts of kindness and mercy to a few months in a given year. Quite the contrary. At Yale, and numerous other colleges and universities throughout the nation, spiritual awakenings were replete throughout the first four decades of the nineteenth century. Yale, for example, was visited by another awakening in 1808 that saw no less than thirty student converts.[23] And between 1815 and 1841 there were twelve similar periods of revival at the New Haven college. The revival of 1831 is particularly noteworthy, for it was said to be the most far-reaching in the history of Yale, in which there were seventy-four conversions on campus and nine hundred in the surrounding community of New Haven.[24]

During this same era, Princeton College was also impacted by revival. Prior to this awakening in the winter of 1815, scarcely a dozen of the more than one hundred students on campus professed personal faith in Jesus Christ. The impact of the revival was recorded in the following description by one who was an eyewitness. There were, he wrote, "some seventy or eighty young men under the influence of deep religious feeling, about forty-five whom were rejoicing in Christ." According to the records, as many as thirty of those converted followed the lead of their brothers at Yale and embraced a call to vocational ministry.[25] The revival came:

> ...without any unusual occurrence in providence, without any alarming event, without any extraordinary preaching, without special instruction, or rather means that might be supposed peculiarly adapted to interest the mind. The divine influences seemed to descend like the silent dew of heaven; and in about four weeks, there were very few individuals in the College edifice who were not deeply impressed with a sense of the importance of spiritual and eternal things. There was scarcely a room—perhaps not one—which was not a place of earnest secret devotion.[26]

Gatherings to pray specifically for revival—known as concerts of prayer—were registered at Brown University in Rhode Island, Yale in Connecticut, Harvard in Massachusetts and Middlebury in Vermont throughout 1815. The fruit of such prayers were eight powerful revivals within a twenty-six-year period at Williams College.[27] The most notable of them was the one that commenced in 1805, the very year that Samuel J. Mills (1783–1818) entered as a freshman. The Holy Spirit had a unique calling for this young man. It was while Mills was a student at Williams College that he was burdened by God through the historic Haystack prayer meeting (1806) to organize the "Society of Brethren," which would be a catalyst in the start of the American Protestant missionary movement.[28] Mills would later play a significant role in the founding of the American Board of Commissioners for Foreign Missions

(1810), which sent Adoniram Judson (1788–1850) and Luther Rice (1783–1836) to Calcutta in 1812.

At Hampden-Sydney College there was also revival. The episode noted earlier in this chapter that illustrated the degenerate spiritual life at this college was, in fact, the very incident used by the Holy Spirit to spark the fires of revival at this eastern institution.[29] Three students exercising their faith in the privacy of their dorm room were surrounded by agnostic peers who demanded they cease their personal acts of devotion. The disturbance grew so severe that the president, Dr. John Blair Smith, was called to investigate. When he realized that the charges against the young men were the "sins" of private worship and prayer, he replied with tears: "Oh, is there such a state of things in this college? Then God has come near to us. My dear young friends, you shall be protected. You shall hold your next prayer meeting in my parlour, and I will be one of your number." Amazingly, half the college was at that meeting and what one nineteenth-century writer termed a "glorious revival" swept not only the college, but the surrounding countryside as well.[30]

Bowdoin College was perhaps the last place that Professor Smyth, his colleagues or many of the believing townspeople ever thought the Spirit of God could reach. *The Princeton Review*, however, reported a different perspective. In the January 1859 issue of this journal it was noted that upon Bowdoin College "the Spirit was from time to time poured out, and has continued to be vouchsafed with increasing frequency and power, especially since the year 1825." This claim was substantiated by the fact that nearly twenty-five per cent of Bowdoin College graduates in 1850 "had become ministers of the Gospel."[31]

Prior to the 1834 awakening at Wake Forest Institute, North Carolina, only a quarter of the student body professed personal faith in Christ. After the flames of the revival fires had softened to a warm glow, fully seventy-five percent of the student body were professing Christians, with half of those remaining "concerned about salvation." Other southern colleges were similarly impacted by such blessings. For example, "nearly all the young men" at

Randolph-Macon College in Virginia were affected in the awakening of 1834, as were a number of the women at the Wesleyan College in Georgia five years later. Two additional Georgian institutions, Mercer University and Cave Springs School, likewise knew spiritual awakening. Mercer shut down all classes and academic pursuits for several days when a "revival burst forth" in 1839, while the students at Cave Springs bypassed exams for an entire week so that they might attend "exclusively to the soul's interest."[32]

Similar times of spiritual fervour were seen at Centre College in Kentucky, Athens in Georgia, Dickinson in Pennsylvania, Dartmouth and Amherst.[33] An awakening was inspired at Marietta in Ohio through the boldness of a student who openly opposed the reading of "infidel works" in a classroom.[34] At another Ohio institution, Denison, revival came as a result of a quiet request for prayer during the what some described as the "dull routine" of a chapel service.[35] Approximately thirty students from Union College in Schenectady, New York, were won to Christ at the funeral service of a departed friend. These professions of faith were part of a great work of grace in that community in which not less than eight hundred souls were hopefully converted.[36]

A fitting conclusion to this chapter might be found in the words of a gentleman who witnessed a revival at the University of Wooster during this era in which fifty students were brought from "darkness to light." Reflecting on this revival, he commented: "A revival in college is an unspeakable blessing; it is so wide-reaching in its influence."[37] What he clearly had in mind was the fact that where else, but on the college and university campus, do many of the future leaders of every nation at some time walk?

For reflection

You've just read some stories that seem too good to be true. I'm not referring to the Cave Spring School exams that were postponed for a week in 1839! I am speaking about stories of God visiting campuses across the nation in such powerful ways that, like Princeton in 1815, nearly every dorm room was found to be a place of earnest secret devotion. It has happened, and could happen again! As a way of preparing for such an awakening, read over the following questions and answer them truthfully:

1. S.E. Morison described the typical student during this general period as "an atheist in religion, an experimentalist in morals, a rebel to authority." In a sentence, write a description of the typical student at your school.

2. Allow me to go one step deeper. If indeed God did come to your school this very year in revival and spiritual awakening, what would he find happening within the private lives of the typical Christian students on your campus? Compare this description with your own private life. What are you like when no one is watching (though God sees your every thought and deed)?

3. When revival came in the early nineteenth century, what transpired spiritually in a few short weeks surpassed all the best efforts of the believing community in years of dutiful service. Scoffers were converted by the score, the believing community was noticeably renewed and the heart of the individual Christian was sanctified afresh to the Lordship of Christ. Do you recall the letter written by a Yale College tutor by the name of Benjamin Silliman, who described what a campus was like that had experienced the footprints of God? He said, "Yale college is a little temple: prayer and praise seem to be the delight of the greater part of the students while those who are still unfeeling are awed into respectful silence." If God chose, he could also walk on your campus in an extraordinary way as he did in the early nineteenth century. What could you do to prepare the way for such an awakening?

For further study

The believing community rapidly deteriorates when its undisputed Lord, Jesus Christ the immortal King, receives neither the homage nor the obedience from those who have pledged allegiance to his Name. Revival, in both wonderful and fearful ways, awakens Christians to the truth that Christ forever and always will be their undisputed Lord! Such was the conviction of Timothy Dwight who, in the following message entitled The Character of Christ, as a King,[38] *supplies keen biblical insights as to the vast dominion of Christ's rule, as well as the duties and blessings of all his subjects. Read his message and answer the following questions:*

a. If Christ is rightly termed King, what is the kingdom over which he rules?

b. How does Christ defend his kingdom?

c. What benefits does Christ give to those who have embraced his rule as their King?

d. What two implications does Dwight see in what he has said about the kingship of Christ?

e. What personal application can you make of this message by Timothy Dwight?

A sermon by Timothy Dwight:
The Character of Christ, as a King

> Which he wrought in Christ, when he raised him from the
> dead, and set *him* at his own right hand in the heavenly *places*,
> Far above all principality, and power, and might, and domin-
> ion, and every name that is named, not only in this world, but
> also in that which is to come: And hath put all *things* under his
> feet, and gave him *to be* the head over all *things* to the church.
> (Ephesians 1:20–22, KJV)

In the text we are presented with several interesting particulars
concerning the kingly office of Christ, which shall now be the subject
of our consideration. We are taught in this passage:

1. *That God hath exalted Christ to this dominion.*
2. *The extent of this kingdom.*
3. *That this kingdom was given, and assumed, for the benefit of
   the Church.*

1. We are taught that God hath exalted Christ to this dominion.
This doctrine is repeatedly taught in the text, in the following
expressions. He set him at his own right hand in the heavenly
places. He hath put all things under his feet. He gave him to be
head over all things. In these expressions the exaltation of Christ to
the dominion and dignity, ascribed to him in the text, is as unequivocally attributed to the Father, as it can be in human language.

2. We are taught the extent of this kingdom.
a) The kingdom of Christ is the universe.
In the text, the extent of Christ's kingdom is repeatedly denoted by
the phrase "all things." The absolute universality of this phrase is
sufficiently manifest from the text itself, when it is said, that he is
set at the right hand of God, far above all principality, and power,
and might, and dominion, and every name that is named in this

world, and that which is to come. But it is placed beyond all doubt in the corresponding passage in Philippians 2:10, where it is said, that "every knee should bow, of *things* in heaven, and *things* in the earth, and *things* under the earth; and *that* every tongue should confess, that Jesus Christ is Lord." Every knee in this vast dominion, we are assured, will one day bow to Christ; and every tongue found in it will confess, at a future period, that Christ is Lord. In the same manner, in Colossians 1:16, all things are said to be created by him, and for him; whether they be visible or invisible, whether in heaven or in earth. As in this absolutely universal sense they were made by and for himself; so from this passage we cannot doubt, that in the same sense they will be his absolute possession. This world, therefore, the planetary system, the stellary systems, the highest heavens above and hell beneath, are all included, and alike included, in the immense empire, of which he is the head.

b) His authority over this great kingdom is supreme.
The whole course of providence is under his immediate control. He upholds all things by the word of his power (Hebrews 1:3); and directs them with universal and irresistible agency to their proper ends. The affairs of this world, and all its inhabitants, are directed by his hand. He has the keys of hell and of death, or of the world of departed spirits (Revelation 1:18).

In the exercise of this dominion he will, at the close of this providential system, summon the dead from the grave, consume the world with fire and judge both the righteous and the wicked, both angels and men (Revelation 20:11–15). In the exercise of the same authority, also, he will send the wicked down to the regions of darkness, and punish them with an everlasting destruction from his presence, and from the glory of his power.

3. We are taught that this kingdom was given for the benefit of the church.
a) Christ defends this kingdom from all his enemies.
The enemies of the Christians are their temptations, internal and external, their sins, death, evil men and evil angels.

Against their temptations, he furnishes them with defense by all the instructions, precepts, warnings reproofs, threatenings and promises which are contained in his Word. These constitute a continual and efficacious protection from the influence of the lusts within and the enemies without by awakening in the soul solemn consideration; alarming it with affecting apprehensions; encouraging it with hope; alluring it with love and gratitude; stimulating it with prospect of a glorious reward; and thus prompting it to watch against the rising sin, to oppose with vigour the intruding temptation, and to pray unceasingly for that divine assistance, which every one that asketh shall receive.

To the means of defense, furnished by his Word, he adds continually the peculiar influences of his Spirit. This glorious Agent, commissioned by Christ for this divine purpose, diffuses through the soul the spirit of resistance, the hope of victory, the strength necessary to obtain it and the peace and joy which are its happy as well as unfailing consequences.

From their sins, he began to deliver them by his atonement. This work he carries on by his intercession (Hebrews 7:25) and completes by his providence. In the present world where all things are imperfect, this deliverance partakes, it must be acknowledged, of the common nature: yet it is such, as to secure them from every fatal evil; and such as to be one of those things, which work together for their good. Their progress towards perfect holiness is slow, irregular and interrupted. Yet it is real and important, and produces hope, comfort and perseverance unto the end.

At the Judgment, this deliverance will be complete. There the glorious effects of his atonement and intercession will be all realized. Everyone of his followers will find himself entirely interested in them both and will see, at that trying period, all his sins washed away and nothing left to be laid to his charge. These dreadful enemies, at this dreadful season, will be powerless and overthrown, and Christians will be more than conquerors through him that hath loved them (Romans 8:37).

The triumphing of the wicked is short. The upright shall have dominion over them in the morning. When Christians are redeemed from the power of the grave, they shall see all these enemies retiring behind them and speedily vanishing, with the flight of ages, to a distance, immeasurable by the power of the imagination. All around them will then be friends. God will then be their Father, angels their brethren, happiness their portion, heaven their ever-lasting home.

b) Christ bestows on Christians all good, temporal and eternal.
Of temporal good, he gives them all that is necessary or useful for such beings in such a state. The world may be and often is a vale of tears and life a solitary pilgrimage through a weary land. Poverty may betide, afflictions befall, diseases arrest and death, at what they may think an untimely period, summon them away. By enemies they may be surrounded and by friends forsaken. They may be exposed to hatred and persecution. Their days may be overcast with gloom and their nights with sorrow. But he has assured them, and they will find the assurance verified, that these are light afflictions which only work for them an eternal weight of glory (2 Corinthians 4:17), and that these, as truly as all other things, work together for their good. Even these, therefore, however forbidding their aspect, will be found to be good for them: good upon the whole; good in such a sense, as to render their whole destiny brighter, better and more happy.

In the mean time, he furnishes them also abundantly with spiritual good. He furnishes them with the sanctification of the soul. He gives them light to discover their own duty, and his glory and excellency. He gives them strength to resist temptations; sorrow for their sins; patience, resignation, and fortitude under afflictions; faith to confide in him and to overcome the world; hope to encourage their efforts and to fix them firmly in their obedience; peace to hush the tumults of the mind and to shed a cheerful serenity over all its affections; and joy to assure them of his glorious presence and to anticipate in their thoughts the everlasting joy of his immortal kingdom.

In the future world, when death shall have been swallowed up in victory and all tears shall be wiped away from their eyes, he will begin to bestow upon them eternal good. In this fullness of joy, everything will be only delightful. Their bodies, raised from the grave in incorruption, power and glory, will be spiritual, immortal, ever vigorous and ever young. Their souls, purified from every stain, and luminous with knowledge and virtue, will be images of his own amiableness and consummate beauty. Their stations, allotments and employment, will be such as become those who are kings and priests in the heavenly world. Their companions will be cherubim and seraphim, and their home will be the house of their Father and their God.

At the same time, in bestowing all this good he himself is both the dispenser and the good dispensed. I, says Christ, am the light of the world (John 8:12). The city, says St. John, had no need of the sun, neither of the moon, to shine in it; for the glory of God did lighten it, and the Lamb is the light thereof (Revelation 21:23). In other words, Christ is the medium through which all the knowledge of God is conveyed to the intelligent universe, his character discovered and his pleasure made known. Of the heavenly world, particularly, he is here expressly declared to be the light: the glory of God did lighten it and the Lamb is the light thereof. The Lamb is not only the dispenser of knowledge, but the thing known; not only the communicator of enjoyment, but the thing enjoyed; the person divinely seen, loved, worshipped and praised for ever. In his presence, all his followers and all their happy companions with open face, beholding in him as in a glass, the glory of the Lord, will be changed into the same image from glory to glory, as by the Spirit of the Lord.

4. Implications
a) From such observations, the divinity of Christ can be conclusively argued.
From the text and the comments here given on it, it is evident that Christ holds the sceptre of the universe and rules the great kingdom of God. Let me ask, who, but the infinitely perfect One, can possibly hold such a sceptre or control successfully, or even at all, such

an empire? Unless he be everywhere present, how can he every-where act, rule and bring to pass such events as he chooses, such as are necessary to the divine glory and the universal good? Unless he is present, acting and ruling everywhere, how can he prevent the existence of such things as will be injurious to this good or fail to be disappointed of his own purposes and ultimately of the supreme end of all his labours? How evident is it, even to our view, that inanimate things must cease to operate and to move in their destined course; that animated beings must wander out of it; and that rational beings must, if virtuous, go astray from the defectiveness of their imperfect nature and, if sinful, from malignity and design. The evil designs of the latter must particularly, if he be not present, multiply in their numbers and increase in their strength until various parts of this immense kingdom become disordered and perhaps destroyed. What an impression would it make on the feelings, what a change in the affairs of this world, if mankind, if evil Spirits, were to know that the ruler of all things would be absent from it, even for a single year! What courage would sinners gather! With what strength and to what a multitude would sins accumulate! What a tempest of violence would ravage this globe! To what a mountainous height would be heaped up the mass of human misery!

Nor is his absolute knowledge of all things less indispensable, than his universal presence. This knowledge is completely necessary to enable him to discern the ends deserving of his pursuit and the proper means of their accomplishment. When all these are resolved on, only the same knowledge can direct the operations of these means, prevent their disorder or their failure, preclude successful opposition and avoid the consequent confusion, distur-bance and disappointment.

By the same knowledge only is the same exalted person qualified to be the final judge and rewarder of the universe. A great part of the sin and holiness of created beings and of the enhancements and diminutions of both lies altogether in their thoughts and volitions. To judge his creatures justly, then, it is absolutely necessary, that he should search the heart of every rational being.

Nor is omnipotence less necessary for all these vast and innumerable purposes than omniscience and omnipresence. No power, inferior to omnipotence, could produce or hold together so many beings, or carry on to completion so many and so various purposes. To the power, actually exerted for these ends, every being must be completely subjected. And all created power must be entirely subordinate. An absolute and irresistible dominion must be exercised unceasingly over every part of his kingdom, or the great designs of creation and providence must be in continual danger of being finally frustrated.

Equally necessary is infinite rectitude for the just, benevolent and perfect administration of such a government. The least defect, the least wrong, would here be fatal. From the decision there can be no appeal. From the arm of execution there can be no escape. A creature, if wronged here, is wronged hopelessly and forever. The ruling Mind must, therefore, be subject to no weakness, passion or partiality. Without perfect rectitude there can be no ultimate confidence, and without such confidence, voluntary, or virtuous, obedience cannot exist.

Thus, when Christ is exalted to be head over all things, and constituted the ruler, judge and rewarder of the universe, he is plainly exalted to a station, which so far as reason can discern, he is unqualified to fill. But he was exalted to this station by unerring and boundless wisdom. Of course, he certainly possesses all the qualifications which it can demand. In other words, he is a person literally divine.

b) From the same observations we may discern how greatly we need such a friend as Christ.

That we are creatures wholly dependent, frail, ignorant, exposed and unable to protect ourselves or provide for our interests, needs neither proof nor illustration. To us, the future is all blank. Between our present existence and the approaching vastness of being hangs a dark and impenetrable cloud. What is beyond it no human eye is able to discern and no human foresight to conjecture. There, however, all our great concerns lie, and are every moment increasing in their number and importance. There we shall enjoy the exquisite emotions and the high dignity of immortal virtue; the pure pleasures of a serene, self-approving mind; the eternal interchange of esteem and affection with the general assembly of the first-born; and the uninterrupted favour of God in the world of joy. Or we shall suffer unceasingly the anguish of a guilty, self-ruined soul; the malignity of evil men and evil angels; and the wrath of our offended Creator in the regions of woe. Between these infinitely distant allotments there is no medium, no intervening state, to which those, who fail of final approbation, can betake themselves for refuge. When, therefore, we bid adieu to this world, we shall meet with events, whose importance nothing but omniscience can estimate.

While we wander through the wilderness of life, amid so many wants, how desirable must it be to find a friend, able and willing, to furnish the needed supplies! Amid so many enemies and dangers, how desirable must it be to find a friend, able and willing to furnish the necessary protection! Amid so many temptations, to watch over us; amid so many sorrows, to relieve us; in solitude, to be our companion; in difficulties, our helper; in despondence, our support; in disease, our physician; in death, our hope, resurrection, and life! In a word, how desirable must it be to find a friend, who, throughout all the strange, discouraging state of present life, will give us peace, consolation and joy, and cause all things, even the most untoward and perplexing, to work together for our good!

On a dying bed especially, when our flesh and our hearts must fail, our earthly friends yield us little consolation and no hope, and the world itself retire from our view; how delightful will such a friend be! Then the soul, uncertain, alone, and stretching its wings for its flight into the unknown vastness, will sigh and pant for an arm on which it may lean, and a bosom on which it may safely recline. But there, Christ is present with all his tenderness and all his power. With one hand he holds the anchor of hope and with the other he points the way to heaven.

In the final resurrection, when the universe shall rend asunder and the elements of this great world shall rush together with immense confusion and ruin, how supporting, how ravishing, will it be when we awake from our final sleep and ascend from the dust in which our bodies have been so long buried to find this glorious Redeemer re-fashioning our vile bodies like unto his glorious body and reuniting them to our minds, purified and immortal (1 Corinthians 15:51–54)! With what emotions shall we arise and stand and behold the Judge descend in the glory of his Father with all his holy angels! With what emotions shall we see the same unchangeable and everlasting friend placing us on his right hand in glory and honour, which kings will covet in vain and before which all earthly grandeur shall be forgotten (Matthew 25:31–33)! With what melody will the voice of the Redeemer burst on our ears, when he proclaims, "Come, ye blessed of my Father, inherit the Kingdom, prepared for you from the foundation of the world" (Matthew 25:34)! How will the soul distend with transport, when accompanied by the church of the first-born, and surrounded by thrones, principalities and powers, it shall begin its flight towards the highest heavens, to meet his Father and our Father, his God and our God (1 Thessalonians 4:15–18)! What an internal heaven will dawn in the mind when we shall be presented before the throne of Jehovah and settled amid our own brethren in our immortal inheritance and our final home, and behold all our sins washed away, our trials ended, our dangers escaped, our sorrows left behind us, and our reward begun, in the world, where all things are ever new, delightful, and divine (Revelation 21:1–5)!

At these solemn and amazing seasons, how differently will those unhappy beings feel, who on a deathbed find no such friend; who rise to the resurrection of damnation; who are left behind when the righteous ascend to meet their Redeemer; who are placed on the left hand at the final trial; and to whom, in the most awful language which was ever heard in the universe, he will say, "Depart from me, ye cursed, into everlasting fire, prepared for the devil and his angels" (Matthew 25:41)!

Timothy Dwight

Timothy Dwight (1752–1817), grandson of the eminent Jonathan Edwards (1703–1758), was born in Northampton, Massachusetts. Amazingly precocious, Dwight entered Yale College at the age of thirteen, graduating in 1769. He became a college tutor in 1771. Between 1778 and 1783 he studied theology with his uncle, Jonathan Edwards, Jr. (1745–1801). In 1783 he became pastor of the Congregational church at Greenfield Hill, Connecticut. During his pastorate he became famous throughout New England for his preaching and for the superb private school that he established close to his church. In 1795, when the presidency of Yale College became vacant, Dwight consented to accept this prestigious position and was inaugurated later that same year. Throughout his term of service the College experienced four distinct periods of spiritual awakening. He was a key leader of the Second Great Awakening. His Yale Chapel sermons were published as the five-volume *Theology Explained and Defended (1818–1819)*, which went through no less than twelve editions in the United States alone.

Resources

For two recent detailed studies of Dwight's life and thought, see Annabelle S. Wenzke, *Timothy Dwight (1752–1817)* (Lewiston/Queenston/Lampeter: Edwin Mellen Press, 1989) and John R. Fitzmier, *New England's Legislator: Timothy Dwight, 1752–1817* (Bloomington/Indianapolis, Indiana: Indiana University Press, 1998).

Engraving of Timothy Dwight, from Timothy Dwight, *Theology Explained and Defended in a Series of Sermons*, vol. 1 (New York: Harper & Brothers, 1867), frontispiece.

1   For a message by Dwight entitled *The Character of Christ, as a King*, see the conclusion of this chapter.

2   *Autobiography, Correspondence, Etc. of Lyman Beecher, D.D.*, ed. Charles Beecher (New York: Harper & Brothers, 1864), II, 43.

3   T.J. Wertenbaker, *Princeton: 1746–1896* (Princeton, New Jersey: Princeton University Press, 1946), 137.

4   Wertenbaker, *Princeton*, 156.

5   S.E. Morison, *Three Centuries of Harvard, 1636–1936* (Cambridge, Massachusetts: Harvard University Press, 1936), 185.

6   A.B. Strickland, *The Great American Revival* (Cincinnati: Standard Press, 1934), 33. For a brief account of Ware's career, see "Ware, Henry" in *Dictionary of Christianity in America*, ed. Daniel G. Reid (Downers Grove, Illinois: InterVarsity Press, 1990), 1233–1234.

7   Clarence P. Shedd, *Two Centuries of Student Christian Movements* (New York: Association Press, 1934), 48.

8   Shedd, *Two Centuries*, 35.

9   Shedd, *Two Centuries*, 41.

10   Shedd, *Two Centuries*, 80.

11   Benjamin Rice Lacy, Jr., *Revivals in the Midst of the Years* (1943 ed.; repr. Hopewell, Virginia: Royal Publishers, Inc., 1968), 70.

12   Shedd, *Two Centuries*, 35.

13   "Religion in Colleges," *The Princeton Review* 31, No.1 (January 1859), 41.

14   F. Rudolph, *The American College and University* (New York: Knopf, 1962), 79.

15   Fred W. Hoffman, *Revival Times in America* (Boston: W.A. Wilde Co., 1956), 66.

16   Shedd, *Two Centuries*, 36.

17   Strickland, *Great American Revival*, 40.

18   Strickland, *Great American Revival*, 36.

19   Strickland, *Great American Revival*, 59.

20   Strickland, *Great American Revival*, 59.

21   H.B. Wright, *Two Centuries of Christian Activity at Yale* (New York: G.P. Putnam's Sons, 1901), 65.

22   "Religion in Colleges," 42.

23   Strickland, *Great American Revival*, 73.

24   Wright, *Two Centuries of Christian Activity*, passim.

25   Lacy, *Revivals*, 93.

26   Joshua Bradley, *Accounts of Religious Revivals in Many Parts of the United States from 1815–1818* (Wheaton, Illinois: Richard Owen Roberts Publishers, 1980), 252–253.

27   Strickland, *Great American Revival*, 75.

28   T.C. Richards, *Samuel J. Mills* (Boston, New York: The Pilgrim Press, 1906), 26–35.

29 See p.27.

30 C.L. Thompson, *Times of Refreshing, A History of American Revivals from 1740–1877* (Chicago: J.S. Goodman, 1877), 79.

31 "Religion in Colleges," 41–42.

32 A. Godbold, *The Church College of the Old South* (Durham: Duke University Press, 1944), 128–138.

33 Lacy, *Revivals*, 95; William Warren Sweet, *The Story of Religion in America* (New York/London: Harper and Brothers, 1930, 1939), 326–327.

34 Rudolph, *American College and University*, 81.

35 G.W. Chessman, *Denison: The Story of an Ohio College* (Grandville, Ohio: Denison University, 1957), 81.

36 W.F.P. Noble, *A Century of Gospel Work* (Philadelphia: H.C. Watts & Co/San Francisco: Al Bancroft & Co., 1876), 295.

37 Noble, *Century of Gospel Work*, 534.

38 This sermon has been edited and abridged for this current work, but can be found in its complete form in Timothy Dwight, *Theology Explained and Defended in a Series of Sermons* (New York: Harper, 1846).

3

A "wonderful revival of religion"

Mid-nineteenth century campus revivals

The setting

As noted in the previous chapter, the cultural environment preceding the Great Awakening was characterized by vast spiritual and moral decline. So it was during the years preceding the mid-century awakening detailed in this chapter. A blunt analysis of this time period by J. Edwin Orr, a historian of revival, affirmed that "between 1845 and 1855, there were several years in which the number of church accessions scarcely kept pace with severe losses."[1] It would, however, be inaccurate to believe that this era of history, or any era for that matter, was entirely void of spiritual life. In every year, at the local level, there were small fires that the Holy Spirit ignited at isolated towns and campuses across the nation. For example, a "revival was in progress" at Randolph-Macon College in 1852.[2] Williams College, which had a tradition of collegiate awakenings, recorded awakenings in 1851 and 1853.[3] History records 1851 as the year that the first Young Men's Christian Association (YMCA), an organization destined to impact college and university campuses throughout the nineteenth century and beyond, was begun in America.[4] Students at Amherst were also among the favoured few who experienced spiritual renewal during this decade of spiritual decline.[5]

Actual spiritual awakenings in the decade between 1845 and 1855 were, however, apparently very few. Moreover, Christians were not alone in yearning for some type of blessing. They were joined by businessmen across the nation whose financial ledgers indicated little to celebrate. According to historian F.G. Beardsley:

> In the autumn of 1857 the country was visited with a severe financial panic, caused by excessive railroad building, over-speculation and a wildcat currency system....A crash was inevitable. When it came, merchants by the thousands all over the country were forced to the wall, banks failed and railroads went into bankruptcy. The financial ruin of the country seemed complete....Many factories were shut down and vast multitudes were thrown out of employment. In New York City alone thirty thousand lost employment on account of these stringent conditions.[6]

Adding to the confusion of this time was the declaration of William Miller (1782–1849), the founder of the Adventist movement, who authoritatively predicted the return of Christ in 1843 and was led, against his better judgement, to make a similar prediction for 1844, when the second coming did not materialize in 1843. The publicity and subsequent adherents to this announcement was widespread, as was the disillusion with Christianity as the claims failed to materialize.[7] In addition, the heightened moral tensions surrounding the issue of slavery, along with the political unrest which eventually gave birth to the Civil War, were further forces influencing both mind and heart.

With rare exception, the collegiate community during this general era was also morally handicapped by the effects of political, financial and spiritual decay. For example, it was said of the pupils at Franklin College that within this Indiana school "drunkenness came second in frequency among all the crimes committed...the indeterminate charge of disorderly conduct coming first."[8] To the abhorrence of a few devout faculty and students, chapel services were frequently disrupted by pranks, vandalism, blatant disrespect, an instance of dancing in the aisle during prayers and, as an expression of student jubilation at the conclusion of services, "bursting torpedoes"![9]

The students at Davidson College in North Carolina, with little knowledge that revival would come to their campus in April 1858, habitually scoffed at the most fundamental of religious expressions. One student observed in 1841 that when grace was said at mealtime, by the time that the "amen was said not a biscuit was left on the plates."[10] At Illinois College, Thomas Beecher, a junior and brother to the president of the institution, was suspended for "repeated disorders tending to disturb the worship of God in Chapel."[11] At Washington College in Maryland it was the son of the school president who was "examined and reprimanded" for disorderly conduct during the same era, while several of the more riotous students were disciplined for shooting pistols on that same campus.[12]

It is sad to note that some of the colleges blessed with revivals during the early years of the century had all but forgotten their former experiences of grace. For instance, various chapel services in the 1850s at Williams College "were characterized by deliberate absenteeism, indifference, disrespect; by ogling female visitors, the writing of obscene doggerel on the flyleaves of hymnals, by expectorating in the chapel aisle."[13] A young man at Randolph-Macon College, a school similarly awakened by God's Spirit in 1834, was found "prostrated on the forest's bosom by the unseemly and unmerciful hand of King Alcohol."[14]

Numerous other illustrations of spiritual desperation could be given, but these suffice to indicate that by mid-century conditions once again were ripe for revival. That revival came in 1857, when enough good news was reported for one historian to classify this mid-century awakening as "the event of the century."[15]

The prayer meeting revival of 1858–1859

In this mid-century awakening, it was an "unknown" by the name of Jeremiah Calvin Lanphier (1809–c.1890) who was instrumental in beginning a prayer meeting that was the catalyst for the Third Great Awakening. Lanphier had worked much of his life in New

Charles Finney (1792–1875),
an important figure in the Second
Great Awakening

York City as a merchant. In 1842, at the age of thirty-three, he was converted in the Broadway Tabernacle, which had been built for Charles Finney (1792–1875). Fifteen years later he relinquished all ties to business and embraced a calling to serve full-time as a lay missionary with the North Reformed Protestant Dutch Church, which was affiliated with the Dutch Reformed denomination.

His burden was to reach the surrounding community of lower New York City. Faced with a challenge that was indeed overwhelming, Lanphier decided to enlist the prayers of others through a weekly noonday prayer meeting. A promotional leaflet was distributed widely throughout the community, with the doors of the North Dutch Church opening at noon on September 23, 1857 for the first formal assembly. He prayed alone until 12:30, at which time he was joined by half a dozen others. The following Wednesday the six intercessors had become twenty. Within six months, an estimated ten thousand businessmen throughout New York City were gathering for *daily* noonday prayer! Only the Holy Spirit of God can have brought this to pass from the meagre efforts of a layman.[16]

Other cities in the United States saw similar prayer meetings come into existence. Believers in Philadelphia and Boston were prompted to assemble for intercession, as were Christians in Chicago, Pittsburgh and Cincinnati. A visitor at a Boston gathering illustrated the breadth of this historic prayer movement through the following testimony: "I am from Omaha, in Nebraska. On my journey east I have found a continuous prayer meeting all the way. We call it two thousand miles from Omaha to Boston; and here was a prayer meeting about two thousand miles in extent."[17]

What harvest resulted from this two thousand miles of prayer? Of the two hundred or so towns in New York State who reported phenomenal outpourings of the Spirit, around six thousand individuals were converted. New Jersey, Pennsylvania, Indiana and Illinois witnessed a collective yield of nearly twenty thousand. The work of grace in Maryland generated some ten thousand conversions, with twelve thousand specified in Ohio. States more sparsely populated such as Michigan, Iowa, Wisconsin, Minnesota and Missouri were blessed in like proportion to their eastern neighbours, while southern states were similarly impacted.[18]

Numerous colleges and universities also experienced the fullness of this mid-century visitation. For example, W.C. Conant, who published a volume in 1858 titled *Narrative of Remarkable Conversions*, records that "the revival in Yale College is probably without a precedent, as far as numbers are concerned." In fact, Conant indicated that the scope of the mid-century awakening at Yale "is said to include nearly all the students; among the converts are some who have been very bitter scoffers, and who were tolerably well aroused with the philosophy of the infidel."[19]

Similarly, the students at Amherst College were consumed with a "wonderful revival of religion" that rested upon the campus like a cloud until the "entire collegiate community was brought under its influence." Concerning the effect of this 1858 visitation, William A. Stearns, the President of Amherst, wrote: "of the Senior Class but three or four remain who have not openly commenced the Christian Life. Of the Junior Class, but one, and he is a serious inquirer, if not a Christian. Of the Sophomore Class, four or five. Of the Freshman Class, nine or ten."[20]

Awakenings were also in progress at Phillips Academy in Andover where there were not less that fifty conversions. At Brown University it was "some of the most reckless and indifferent students" who embraced personal faith in Christ.[21] In the spring of 1858, Williams College experienced a powerful revival during which, according to one student report, "There are very few who are not deeply interested in the subject of their soul's salvation."[22] And at Jefferson College in Pennsylvania, there were twenty students who professed faith in Christ, while numerous others were "seriously inquiring."[23] Oberlin College in Ohio was not overlooked as *The Oberlin Evangelist* noted that God's Spirit moved "quietly and silently," drawing students to both prayer and personal professions of faith.[24]

The 240 students who united with local churches in Lima, New

York, were part of a "gracious revival of religion" that had occurred at Genesee College. Princeton was also caught in these winds of revival. On the Princeton campus there were over one hundred converts, fifty of whom subsequently went into vocational ministry. Davidson College, known by some as a haven for the drunkard and immoral, in the spring of 1858 became a haven of spiritual rest as around eighty of the one hundred seniors became believers. A score of other campuses across the nation—including Wofford College in South Carolina, Emory University in Georgia, Madison College in Wisconsin, Baylor University in Texas, the University of Michigan and the Ohio schools of Denison, Miami University, Kenyon College, Wilberforce University and Ohio Wesleyan—all experienced similar revivals during this same year. [25]

The expansion

A central vehicle for the expansion of God's work in the latter half of the nineteenth century was the YMCA. This historic association was begun in 1844 by a dozen London clerks in a dry goods establishment for the purpose of "spiritual and mental improvement."[26] The movement spread rapidly throughout Britain and Europe, with an association of great size convening at the famous Exeter Hall in London in January 1859 to hear a young preacher by the name of Charles Haddon Spurgeon "plead the necessity of a revival."[27] The following year much of Europe was experiencing the divine favour that America had known the previous year.[28] The YMCA spread to America through a letter written by a Columbia University student who had studied in Edinburgh and had witnessed first-hand the benefits of the British YMCA. From its inception in 1851 in America to reach troubled inner city youth in Boston to its expansion into the collegiate community in 1858, the American YMCA increased to over 180 college associations by 1884. Born in a season of revival fervour, the initial college associations were generally staffed by student leadership dedicated to evangelism as well as discipling new believers.[29]

D.L. Moody (1837–1899),
the most prominent transatlantic evangelist
of the late nineteenth century

Carleton College in Minnesota, for example, boasted a small but active YMCA group in 1878 with eighteen members. In that year, however, the eighteen multiplied until "every member of the four college classes had taken a stand on the Lord's side."[30] A revival at Princeton in 1876 was described by the YMCA there as "the most remarkable that ever occurred in the history of the institution," with nearly one hundred of the graduating seniors claiming to be "followers of the Lamb."[31] The YMCA groups at the Massachusetts Colleges of Williams and Worchester also reported numerous prayer meetings, evangelistic efforts and conversions throughout this period.[32]

Luther D. Wishard (1854–1925), who was deeply involved in the growth and expansion of the YMCA, was well acquainted with powerful workings of the Spirit within a collegiate setting.[33] While Wishard was a student at Princeton University in 1876, plans had been made for D.L. Moody (1837–1899) to hold a series of revival services on campus. Although Moody was unable to be present in the initial phase of the services, there was a rich outpouring of blessing. "The results were instantaneous," Wishard later wrote, "men by the dozen and by the score began to ask the question of the Philippian jailer," that is, "What must I do to be saved?"[34] When Moody joined the services in the latter part of the week, the number of conversions intensified.

Despite Moody's contact with students in both the States and Europe, he was always aware of his own educational limitations and thus felt that there had to be men better qualified than he was who could bring Christ's message to college students. Moody was not at all a polished speaker. He would pronounce the word "Jerusalem," for instance, with only two syllables! Throughout the latter years of the nineteenth century, however, God used this academically "unqualified" servant to speak to numerous student gatherings. In 1876, for instance, he spoke to eighteen hundred students in Cambridge, England, an event that was instrumental in the conversion of C.T. Studd (1863–1931) and S.P. Smith—two of the famous "Cambridge Seven" who went to China as missionaries

—and countless others. The evident blessing on Moody's ministry at Cambridge opened doors in America for similar ministry at Princeton, Dartmouth and Harvard. These experiences helped to bond the heart of Moody to campus ministry, increasing both his interest and participation.[35]

An outcome of Moody's growing investment in the student movement was the convening of a conference aimed directly at students in the summer of 1886. Wishard had persuaded Moody to hold this conference at Northfield, Massachusetts. As it turned out, 250 students attended the event. Among those present was a young law student from Cornell University in New York by the name of John R. Mott (1865–1955) who, along with a hundred other students, embraced a call to missions. This immediate upsurge in missionary interest led to the development of the Student Volunteer Movement for Foreign Missions. Mott was elected to serve as its chairman. Less than a decade later, the visionary leadership of Wishard and Mott led to a meeting with Christian mission groups in various European countries that resulted in the formation of the World Student Christian Federation. Tens of thousands of students were drawn to missionary service through these organizations whose impact was nothing short of global.[36]

By the turn of the century, the names of Wishard, Moody and Mott, along with the YMCA, Student Volunteer Movement for Foreign Missions and the World Student Christian Federation were familiar to many within the Christian campus community. Consistent spiritual discipleship was likewise commonplace on many American campuses. The stories of *phenomenal* collegiate awakenings were, however, increasingly treasured memories shared by aging alumni. The new generation of college students, for the most part, had yet to experience the seasons of revival. That was soon to change, as we shall see.

For reflection

1. As we have observed, the political, financial and spiritual conditions preceding the mid-nineteenth century awakening in America were deeply distressing. In three or four sentences, summarize the current political, financial and spiritual condition of America.

2. Look deeply into your heart: is your God powerful enough to break through the floundering political, financial and spiritual conditions that are so evident today and bring another spiritual awakening like that of 1858?

3. Write a prayer to God that expresses your sorrow over the sins of your nation and school, along with your earnest, hopeful and humble entreaty for another outpouring of divine grace.

4. In the midst of the awakening of 1858, students at Brown University found the Spirit of God drawing even "some of the most reckless and indifferent students" into the household of faith. Davidson College, which was known as a "harbour for the drunkard and immoral," found that 80% of the senior class either renewed or began their Christian faith in the spring of 1858 when God walked on their campus. Using first names only, create a list which contains several of "the most reckless and indifferent students" on your campus. Take a step further, and invite God to place the name of one or two on your heart so that you might join in regular intercession for their conversion or spiritual renewal.

For further study

Using an unusual text, the following address, Solemn Pleadings for Revival,[37] *was given by Charles Haddon Spurgeon in 1875. It guides the reader toward a deeper understanding of true intercessory prayer. This particular message, as well as the prayers of the author contained within it, needs to be pondered deeply and meditated upon.*

Charles Haddon Spurgeon

Charles Haddon Spurgeon (1834–1892), born in Kelvedon, Essex, was undoubtedly one of the most influential preachers of the nineteenth century. Converted in 1850, he united with the Baptists and preached in various locations until 1854 when he accepted a call to serve New Park Street Chapel, London. Under his masterful preaching and the Spirit of God's sovereign blessing, the work at New Park Street prospered and grew. A new building was soon required—named the Metropolitan Tabernacle—to accommodate crowds of up to six thousand! In 1855 he began to publish his weekly sermons. The following year he founded a pastor's college where nearly nine hundred young men, who were called to Christian service but who were lacking in academic qualifications, were trained by the time of his death.

Resources

For a superb collection of Spurgeon material, see Phil Johnson, "The Spurgeon Archive" at www.spurgeon.org. Also see "Spurgeon Gems" at www.spurgeongems.org. A very readable biography is that of Arnold Dallimore, *Spurgeon: A new biography* (Chicago: Moody Press, 1984). For Spurgeon's own account of his life, see the abridged two-volume version of what was originally a four-volume autobiography: *C.H. Spurgeon: The Early Years, 1834–1859* (London: The Banner of Truth Trust, 1962) and *C.H. Spurgeon: The Full Harvest, 1860–1892* (Edinburgh: The Banner of Truth Trust, 1973).

Charles Spurgeon at age twenty-one.

A sermon by C.H. Spurgeon:
Solemn Pleadings for Revival

> Keep silence before me, O islands; and let the people renew
> *their* strength: let them come near; then let them speak: let
> us come near together to judgment.
> (Isaiah 41:1, KJV)

The text is a challenge to the heathen to enter into a debate with
the living God. The Lord bids them argue at their best and let the
controversy be calmly carried out to its issues, so as to be decided
once for all. He bids them be quiet, reflect, and consider, in order
that with renewed strength they may come into the discussion and
defend their gods if they can. He urges them not to bring flippant
arguments, but such as have cost them thought, and have weight
in them, if such arguments can be. He bids them be quiet till they
are prepared to speak and then, when they can produce their
strong reasons and set their cause in the best possible light, he
challenges them to enter the lists and see if they can maintain for
a moment that their gods are gods, or anything better than deceit
and falsehood.

I am not about to speak of that controversy at this time, but to
use the text with quite another view. We also who worship the
Lord God Most High have a controversy with him. We have not
seen his church and his cause prospering in the world for many a
day as we could desire; as yet heathenism is not put to the rout by
Christianity, neither does the truth everywhere trample down
error; nations are not born in a day; the kingdoms of the world
have not become the kingdoms of our Lord and of his Christ. We
desire to reason with God about this, and he himself instructs us
how to prepare for this sacred debate. He bids us be silent; he bids
us consider, and then draw near to him with holy boldness and
plead with him, produce our cause and bring forth our strong reasons. We have read of wonderful revivals; history records the

prodigies of the Reformation, and the marvellous way in which the gospel was spread during the first two centuries; we pine to see the like again, or to know the reason why it is not so, and with holy boldness it is our desire to come before the Lord and plead with him, as a man pleadeth with his friend. May God help us so to do in the power of the Holy Ghost.

First, then, *let us be silent*. "Keep silence before me, O islands." Before the controversy opens let us be silent with *solemn awe*, for we have to speak with the Lord God Almighty! Let us not open our mouths to impugn his wisdom, nor allow our hearts to question his love. What if things do not look as bright as we could wish? The Lord reigneth. And what if he seems to delay? Is he not the Lord God with whom a thousand years are as one day, and who is not slack concerning his promise as some men count slackness? We are going to make bold to speak with him but still he is the eternal God, and we are dust and ashes. Whatever we may say with holy boldness, we would not utter a word in rash familiarity. He is our Father, but he is our Father in heaven. He is our Friend, but at the same time he is our judge. We know that whatsoever he doeth is best. We would not say unto our Maker, "What makest thou?" nor to our Creator, "What hast thou done?" Shall the potter give account to the clay for the works of his hands? "It is the Lord, let him do what seemeth good."

Our silence of awe should deepen into that of *shame*; for, though it is certainly true that the cause of God has not prospered, whose fault is this? Truly, when I see how God has blessed us, I am not so much astonished that he has not given more, as I am amazed that he has given so much. Does he bless such unworthy instruments, such laggards, such slothful workers? Does he do anything by tools so unfit? Does he place any treasure in vessels so impure? This is to be ascribed to his grace.

Go further than this, and keep the silence of *consideration*. This is a noisy age, and the church of Christ herself is too noisy. We have very little silent worship, I fear. I do not so much regret the absence of silence from the public assembly as from our private devotions, where it has a sacred hallowing influence, unspeakably valuable. Let us be silent, now, for a minute, and consider what is it that we desire of the Lord. The conversion of thousands, the overthrow of error, the spread of the Redeemer's kingdom. Think in your minds what the blessings are which your soul pants after. Get a correct idea of them, and then enquire whether you are prepared to receive them. Suppose they were to be now bestowed, are you ready? If thousands of converts were to be born unto this one church, are you prepared to teach them, instruct them, and comfort them? Are you doing it now, you Christian people? Are you acting in such a way that God knows you to be fit to have the charge of those converts that you are asking for? You pray for grace—are you using the grace you have? You want to see more power—how about the power you have? Are you employing it? If a mighty wave of revival sweeps over London, are your hearts ready? Are your hands ready? Are your purses ready? Are you altogether ready to be carried along on the crest of that blessed wave?

Consider. If you reflect, you will see that God is able to give his church the largest blessing, and to give it at any time. Keep silence and consider, and you will see that he can give the blessing by you or by me; he can make any one of us, weak as we are, mighty through God to the pulling down of strongholds, can make our feeble hands, though we have but a few loaves and fishes, capable of feeding myriads with the bread of life. Have we really a desire for these things, which we say we desire? Could we give up worldly engagements to attend to the work of God? Could we spare time to look after the Lord's vineyard? Are we willing to do the Lord's work; and are we in the state of heart in which we can do it efficiently and acceptably? Keep silence and consider. I would suggest to every Christian that he should sit a while before God when he reaches his home, and worship with the silence of awe, with the silence of shame, and then with the silence of careful thought concerning these things.

Then we shall pass on to the silence of *attention*. "Keep silence before me, O islands": keep silence that God may speak to you;

that God's Word may be heard in your soul; not parts of it only, but all of it; that God's Spirit may be heard with his gentle monitions warning you, with his blessed enlightenments revealing to you yourself and your Lord, with his divine promptings urging you to greater consecration and superior holiness, and with his divine assistance leading you onward in the path of a higher life than you have yet attained. Oh, it is well to sit still before the Lord, deaf to every voice but the divine.

If you have learned attention, be silent with *submission*. For this you will need the gracious aid of the Holy Ghost. It is not easy to attain to full submission of soul to whatsoever the Lord wills. We are often like hard brass which will not take the impression from the seal, but if we were what we should be, we should be as melted wax which at once takes the stamp that is put upon it. Oh, to have a heart that is quite silent as to any wish or will, or opinion, or judgment of our own, so that God's mind shall be our mind, God's will shall be our will. The church would soon be healed of her sorrows, and delivered from her divisions, if she would for a while be silent. Oh, that the church would sit at Jesus' feet, lay aside her prejudices, and take the Word in its simplicity and integrity, and accept what God the Lord, and he only, doth declare to be the truth.

In that silence let us renew our strength. Noise wears us; silence feeds us. To run upon the Master's errands is always well, but to sit at the Master's feet is quite as necessary; for, like the angels which excel in strength, our power to do his commandments arises out of our hearkening to the voice of his Word. If even for a human controversy quiet thought is a fit preparation, how much more is it needful in solemn pleadings with the Eternal One? Now let the deep springs be unsealed; let the solemnities of eternity exercise their power while all is still within us.

But how happens it that such silence renews our strength? It does so, first, by *giving space for the strengthening Word to come into the soul, and the energy of the Holy Spirit to be really felt.* Words, words, words; we have so many words, and they are but chaff, but where is *the Word* that in the beginning was God and was with

God? That Word is the living and incorruptible seed, "What is the chaff to the wheat?" saith the Lord. We want less of the words of man and more of him who is the very Word of God. Be quiet, be quiet, and let Jesus speak. Let his wounds speak to you; let his resurrection speak to you; let his ascension and his subsequent glory speak to you; and let the trumpet of his Second Advent ring in your ears. You cannot hear the music of the wheels of these glorious things because of the rattle of care and the vain jangle of disputatious self-wisdom. Be silent, that you may hear the voice of Jesus, for when he speaks you will renew your strength.

We must be silent to renew our strength, next, by *using silence for consideration as to who it is that we are dealing with.* We are going to speak with God about the weakness of his church and the slowness of its progress. Be silent, that you may remember who he is with whom you are expostulating. It is God the Omnipotent, who can make his church mighty if he will, and that at once. We are coming to plead now with one whose arm is not shortened, and whose ear is not heavy. Renew your strength as you think of him. If you have doubted the ultimate success of Christianity, renew your strength as you remember who it is that has sworn by himself that surely all flesh shall see the salvation of God. You are coming to plead with Jesus Christ. Be silent, and remember those wounds of his with which he has redeemed mankind! Can these fail of their reward? Shall Jesus be robbed of the power he has so dearly earned? The earth is the Lord's, and he will unswathe her of the mists which dimmed her lustre at the fall, and he will make this planet shine as brightly as when she first was rolled from between the palms of the omnipotent Creator. There shall be a new heaven and a new earth, wherein dwelleth righteousness. Think of that, and renew your strength. Hath not the Lord said concerning his beloved Son, that he shall divide the spoil with the strong, and the pleasure of the Lord shall prosper in his hands? Shall it not be so?

Think, too, that you are about to appeal to the Holy Spirit; and there again you have the same divine attributes. What cannot the Spirit of God do? He sent the tongues of fire at Pentecost, and

Parthians, Medes, and Elamites, and men of every nation heard the gospel at once. He turned three thousand hearts by one sermon to know the crucified Saviour to be the Messiah. He sent the apostles like flames of fire through the whole earth, till every nation felt their power. He can do the like again. He can bring the church out of darkness into noonday. Let us renew our strength as we think of this. The work we are going to plead about is not ours one-half so much as it is God's: it is not in our hands, but in hands that cannot fail.

In silence, too, let us renew our strength by *remembering his promises*. We want to see the world converted to God, and he has said that "The knowledge of the Lord shall cover the earth as the waters cover the sea." "The glory of the Lord shall be revealed, and all flesh shall see it together, for the mouth of the Lord hath spoken it." "They that dwell in the wilderness shall bow before him; and his enemies shall lick the dust." "The idols he shall utterly abolish." There are a thousand promises. Let us think of that, and however difficult the enterprise may be, and however dark our present prospects, we shall not dare to doubt when Jehovah has spoken and pledged his word.

Our strength will be renewed, next, if in silence *we yield up to God all our own wisdom and strength*. I never am so full as when I am empty; I have never been so strong as in the extremity of weakness. The source of our worst weakness is our home-born strength, and the source of our worst folly is our personal wisdom. Lord, help us to be still till we have abjured ourselves, till we have said, "Lord, our ways of working cannot be compared with thy ways of working; teach us how to work: Lord, our judgments are weak compared with thy perfect judgment; we are fools, be thou our teacher and guide in all things. Crush out of us our fancied strength, and make us like worms, for it is the worm Jacob that thou wilt make into the new sharp threshing instrument, which shall thresh the mountain." After this sort shall you renew your strength.

Keep silence, then, and renew your strength most gloriously by *casting yourselves upon the strength of God*. More than ever before let your inmost souls be filled with trust in the arm that never fails, the hand that never loses its cunning, the eye that is never closed, the heart that never wavers. Jehovah works everywhere, and all things are his servants. He works in the light, and we see his glory; but he equally works in the darkness, where we cannot perceive him. His wisdom is too profound to be at all times understood of mortal men. Let us be patient and wait his time. With no more doubt of our Father's power than the child at its mother's breast has of its mother's love; with no more doubt than an angel before the throne can have of Jehovah's majesty, let us commit ourselves, each one after his own fashion, to suffering and to labour for the grand cause of God, feeling well assured that neither labour nor suffering can be in vain in the Lord.

Our text proceeds to add, "Then let them draw near." Beloved, you that know the Lord, I would urge upon you to *draw near*. You are silent, you have renewed your strength, now enjoy access with boldness. The condition in which to intercede for others is not that of distance from God, but that of great nearness to him. Even thus did Abraham draw nigh when he pleaded for Sodom and Gomorrah. May God the Holy Spirit draw us near even now. Perhaps the following five considerations may help us in so doing.

Let us remember *how near we really are*. We have been washed from every sin in the precious blood of Jesus; we are covered from head to foot at this moment with the spotless righteousness of Immanuel, God with us; we are accepted in the Beloved; yea, we are at this moment one with Christ, and members of his body. How could we be nearer? How near is Christ to God? So near are we! Come near, then, in your personal pleadings, for you are near in your covenant Representative. The Lord Jesus has taken manhood into union with the divine nature, and now between God and man there exists a special and unparalleled relationship, the like of which the universe cannot present. Come near, then, O ye sons of God, come near, for you are near. Stand where your sonship places you, where your Representative stands on your behalf.

The next consideration which may help you to draw near is that you *are coming to a Father.* That was a blessed word of our Lord's, "The Father himself loveth you." As surely as my earthly father is near akin to me, and I may come to him with loving familiarity, so may I approach the Lord, who hath begotten me again unto a lively hope by the resurrection of Jesus Christ from the dead, and I may say to him, "Abba," "Father," and he will not disregard the cry. Hath he not given us the Spirit of adoption? How can he despise that which he gives? Come, then, and speak in your Father's ear. O child of God, you are not talking to a stranger, you are not about to hold a debate with an enemy, you are not seeking to wring a blessing from an unwilling hand. It is to your Father that you speak. Come near to him, I pray you, and plead this day.

Remember next, that *the desire which is in our heart for God's glory and the extension of his Church, is a desire written there by the Holy Spirit.* Now, if the Holy Spirit himself indites the prayer, and he knows the mind of God, if he makes intercession in our hearts according to the will of God, we need have no hesitation to express our desires, because our desires are simply the shadow of the eternal purpose; and that which always was in the mind of God to give, the Spirit of God has inclined us to ask. True prayer is the intimation of God to man that he intends to bless him. It is the herald of mercy. Plead, then, O child of God, for the Spirit of God is pleading in you. Come and speak out that which he speaks within. When the Spirit prompts, what cause can there be for hesitation?

Remember next, that *what we ask,* if we are now about to plead with God concerning his kingdom, is *according to his own mind.* We are at one with God in this matter. If it were not for God's glory for sinners to be converted we would not pray for it. We desire to see thousands of sinners turn to Christ, but it is with this view that the infinite mercy, wisdom, power and love of God may be manifested towards them, and so God may be praised. Verily, much as our heart is set upon the prosperity of the church of God, if it were conceivable that such prosperity would not glorify God we would not ask for it. We desire to see not our notions, but God's truth prevail. I do not want you to believe as I believe except so far as that belief is according to the mind of God. I pray every believer here to search his heart and see whether his desire be a pure one, having God's glory as its Alpha and Omega. It is God's truth, God's kingdom, God's glory that we want to see promoted. If this be the case may we not come very boldly? We have not only the king's ear but his heart also, and we may open our mouths wide.

I now come to the fourth and last point which is, *"Let us speak."* Be silent, renew your strength, draw near and then speak. Let us first speak in the spirit of *adoring gratitude.* How sweet to think that there should be a Saviour at all; to think that there should be a heavenly kingdom set up, as it is set up; that it should have made such advances as it has made, and should still grow mightily! That Jesus Christ should be seen of angels is put down as a wonder, but it is mentioned next to it that he was "believed on in the world." He has been believed on by millions and, however gloomy the prospects of the church may appear, the kingdom of Christ is not an insignificant kingdom, even now. Those who deride her laugh too soon. She is in her twilight as Voltaire said, but it is the twilight of her morning and not of her evening. Brighter times are coming; but even now, up to this moment, the history of the church cannot be told without adoring gratitude to God. She has been foolish and has lost her strength but, like Samson's, it will return.

Next, let us speak in *humble expostulation.* I would earnestly urge upon my brethren in Christ to expostulate thus with the Lord: "O Lord, thy truth does not prosper in the land, yet thou hast said, 'My word shall not return unto me void.' Lord, thou art every day blasphemed, and yet thou hast said that thy glory shall be seen of all flesh. Lord, they set up the idols; even in this land, where thy martyrs burned, they are setting up the graven images again. Lord, tear them down, for thy name's sake; for thine honour's sake, we beseech thee, do it. Dost thou not hear the enemy triumph? They say the gospel is worn out. They tell us that we are the relics of an antiquated race; that modern progress has swept the old faith away. Wilt thou have it so, good Lord? Shall the gospel be accounted a worn out almanac, and shall they set up their new gospels in its stead? Souls are being lost, O God of mercy! Hell is being filled, O God of infinite compassion! Jesus sees but few brought to himself and washed in his precious blood. Time is flying, and every year increases the number of the lost! How long, O God, how long? Wherefore tarriest thou?" In this manner order your case before the Lord, and he will hearken unto you.

When you have spoken by way of expostulation, then turn to *pleading*. Plead with all your skill in argument. "There is thy promise, O Jehovah; wilt thou not keep it? Thou hast said unto thy Son, 'Ask of me, and I will give thee the heathen for thine inheritance, and the uttermost parts of the earth for thy possession!' We do ask in Jesus' name. Do it for thy promise's sake! Lord, thou hast done great and unspeakable things in times gone by: we have heard with our ears, and our fathers have told us the wondrous things which thou didst in their days and in the old time before them: thou art the same Lord, therefore glorify thyself again. By all the past, we beseech thee, reveal thyself at this present." Plead with the Lord and lay stress upon his glory. Tell him that it glorifies his mercy to save sinners, and glorifies his wisdom and his power, yea, every attribute of his divine nature. Then plead the merit of his Son. Oh brethren, plead the blood, plead the wounds, plead the bloody sweat in Gethsemane, plead the cross, plead the death and resurrection, and come not away from the mercy seat till with this mighty plea you have won the victory.

Again, after we have been silent, after we have renewed our strength, and after we have drawn near to God, let us speak today in the way of *dedication*. Now, here I cannot suggest to any man what he in particular may speak. I charge you before the living God lie not unto him, but if you can say this, I pray you say it: "I give to God this day my whole being, absolutely and forever, my body, my soul, my spirit. I have asked that his kingdom may come: I pledge myself in his sight to extend that kingdom by every power I possess or may be able to gain, by every opportunity he may put in my way and by every means which I am able to use." I will not suggest to any of you more than this, whatever the Lord moves you to do, do it; but I do think when we come to plead with the Lord after this fashion we ought to be able to say, "Lord, do spread thy kingdom. I do for thee all I can. I boast not of it, for all I do I ought to do, and I wish I could do a thousand times as much; but still, Lord, during this year of grace I hope to do much for thee which I may have forgotten hitherto."

Last of all, let us speak still in the way of *confidence*. However we may complain of the spread of error, the deaths of good men, and the fewness of able ministers to take their places; however we may think the times to be dark and dreary, let us never speak as if God were dead. I walked some time ago with one of the most earnest Christians I know of, a very devout man, and he told me he was afraid that one day the streets of London would run with blood. He was afraid of an educated democracy which, being uneducated in religion in school board schools, would become clever atheists, and cast off all reverence for God and law; and he gave me an awful picture of what was going to happen. But I touched him on the arm and said, "There is one thing you have forgotten, dear friend. God is not dead yet. What you are dreading will never occur in this land, I am sure. We have an open Bible, we have still some who preach the gospel with all their hearts, and there is still a salt and leaven in the city of London that God will bless to keep down the rottenness and corruption. In spite of all his foes, the Lord reigneth." What, my friends, the devil conquer our God? Never! That is his ultimatum, the course of hellish craft can go no further. Therefore even now let every heart shout, "Hallelujah, Hallelujah," and yet again let us say, "Hallelujah, the Lord reigneth, and all must be well."

1 J. Edwin Orr, *The Light of the Nations* (Grand Rapids, Michigan: Wm. B. Eerdmans Publishing Co., 1965), 100.

2 A. Godbold, *The Church College of the Old South* (Durham, North Carolina: Duke University Press, 1944), 130.

3 F. Rudolph, *Mark Hopkins and the Log: Williams College, 1836–1872* (New Haven: Yale University Press, 1956), 99.

4 Clarence P. Shedd, *Two Centuries of Student Christian Movements* (New York: Association Press, 1934), 93.

5 F. Rudolph, *The American College and University: A History* (New York: Knopf, 1962), 84.

6 F.G. Beardsley, *A History of American Revivals* (New York: American Tract Society, 1904), 216–217.

7 Orr, *Light of the Nations*, 99.

8 E.M. Coulter, *College Life in the Old South* (Athens, Georgia: University of Georgia Press, 1951), 79.

9 Coulter, *College Life*, 82–83.

10 Godbold, *Church College of the Old South*, 120.

11 Rudolph, *American College*, 75.

12 Godbold, *Church College of the Old South*, 113.

13 Rudolph, *American College*, 76.

14 Godbold, *Church College of the Old South*, 113.

15 J. Edwin Orr, *The Re-Study of Revival and Revivalism* (Pasadena, California: School of World Missions 1981), v.

16 For the story, see J. Edwin Orr, *America's Great Revival* (Elizabethtown, Pennsylvania: McBeth Press, 1957).

17 Beardsley, *History of American Revivals*, 213–228.

18 W.C. Conant, *Narrative of Remarkable Conversions* (New York: Derby and Jackson, 1858), 432–435.

19 Conant, *Narrative of Remarkable Conversions*, 378.

20 *The Oberlin Evangelist* (May 12, 1858).

21 *The Oberlin Evangelist* (May 5, 1858).

22 *The Oberlin Evangelist* (March 31, 1858).

23 *The Oberlin Evangelist* (March 31, 1858).

24 *The Oberlin Evangelist* (March 24, 1858).

25 J. Edwin Orr, *The Event of the Century*, ed. Richard Owen Roberts (Wheaton, Illinois: International Awakening Press, 1989), 182–190.

26 Shedd, *Two Centuries*, 92. On the so-called "Father of the Y.M.C.A.," George Williams (1821–1905), see John Pollock, *A Fistful of Heroes: Great Reformer and Evangelists* (Basingstoke, Hampshire: Marshall Pickering, 1988), 66–73.

27 C.H. Spurgeon, *Revival Year Sermons* (London: The Banner of Truth Trust, 1959), 9.

28 At the close of this chapter the reader will have the opportunity to "hear" again Spurgeon's passion in this regard through a printed sermon entitled *Solemn Pleadings for Revival.*

29 Shedd, *Two Centuries*, 92–167.

30 *The Watchman* (Chicago, Illinois, November 1, 1879), 243.

31 *The Watchman* (Chicago, Illinois, November 1, 1879), initial page.

32 *Y.M.C.A. Quarterly* (May 1868), 94–95.

33 On Wishard, see J.H. Dorn, "Wishard, Luther Deloraine" in *Dictionary of Christianity in America*, ed. Daniel G. Reid (Downers Grove, Illinois: InterVarsity Press, 1990), 1266.

34 L.D. Wishard, "The Beginning of the Students' Era in Christian History" (Unpublished manuscript, 1917, Y.M.C.A. Historical Library), 56.

35 Shedd, *Two Centuries*, 234–236.

36 Shedd, *Two Centuries*, 238–373.

37 This sermon has been edited, but can be found in its entirety in *C.H. Spurgeon's Sermons on Revival*, ed. Charles T. Cook (Grand Rapids, Michigan: Zondervan Publishing House, 1958), 17–30.

4

"Without any human planning"

Campus revivals in the early twentieth century

The setting

Unlike the nineteenth-century awakenings, the 1904–1905 Welsh Revival came to a nation that, for nearly five decades, had known spiritual advancement and relative peace.[1] The Christian leaders and organizations prominent in the 1904–1905 revival were numerous. For example, the ministries of John Wilbur Chapman (1859–1918), Samuel Porter Jones (1847–1906) and Reuben Archer Torrey (1856–1928) expanded in scope and influence during this general era. Jones was a powerful preacher, well-known in the southern States. Chapman participated in evangelistic campaigns within both his own Presbyterian fellowship as well as inter-denominationally.[2] Torrey, the first superintendent of the Moody Bible Institute in Chicago, was destined to fill the founder's pulpit following his death in 1899. During the awakening of the early twentieth century, the evangelistic campaigns of Torrey were to be graced with success "unprecedented since the days of Moody."[3]

The World Student Christian Federation, the Student Volunteer Movement for Foreign Missions and the YMCA continued to flourish under the leadership J.R. Mott, L.D. Wishard and a host of paid and volunteer staff. It was stated that the student associations between 1900 and 1915 went "from strength to strength, increasing in membership, scope of program, and significance in American religious life."[4] Various state universities in the United

Reuben A. Torrey (1856–1928),
an evangelist whose ministry was blessed with revival blessing
in the early twentieth century

States also retained historic ties to the Christian faith, with clergy-men filling the position of president in numerous schools. The turn of the century found "chapel and religious assemblies were general and in many (state) institutions attendance was required."[5]

No one was better known for his or her role in the 1904–1905 awakening than a young student by the name of Evan Roberts (1878–1951). Roberts, who had spent a good part of his life mining coal, was called by God to return to his native Welsh village of Loughor and share the good news of the gospel. Over a series of weeks, and most probably to the surprise of the somewhat timid coal miner, those awakened by the Spirit grew from an initial handful to virtually tens of thousands.[6]

News concerning the marvellous visitation of God to Wales spread through Europe, and then to the world. One visitor from America, a certain A.F. Williamson, commented on "the simplicity of organization and lack of anything superfluous or mechanical in the conduct of the meetings in Wales, the only leader recognized being the Holy Spirit, even the most skeptical being compelled to believe it as genuine."[7] Within a short time, similar awakenings were reported in churches and on campuses throughout Great Britain, Western Europe, Canada, the United States, Australia, New Zealand and South Africa.[8]

The awakening

Revival historian J. Edwin Orr details the wonder and scope of the 1904–1905 visitation of God:

> Despite the lack of any large evangelistic campaign, the churches were obviously in the midst of a revival of greater power and extent than New England had known since 1858. The movement was characterized by an intense sensation of the presence of God in the congregations, as in the Welsh Revival. Despite the lack of organization, either in meetings or follow-up, the movement was deemed most effective com-

pared with organized evangelistic campaigns. Churches large and small, here and there, were affected.[9]

Similar to earlier revivals we have looked at, colleges were also deeply impacted. In fact, a writer for the July 1905 issue of the *Missionary Review of the World* was bold enough to suggest that "never in the history of universities have there been so many genuine spiritual awakenings among students. These have not been confined to Christian colleges and universities; in fact, some of the remarkable revivals have taken place in undenominational and non-Christian universities."[10]

An astonishing ninety percent of the students at the University of Florida, for example, were drawn to the evangelistic meetings led by W.D. Weatherford during the spring semester of 1905.[11] A powerful series of meetings at State College, Pennsylvania, was attended by over 900 men with Christian professions numbering in the hundreds.[12] A number of Virginia institutions, including Randolph-Macon, Henry College and Fork Union Academy, all reported "marked spiritual awakenings."[13] It was through a series of meetings at Oberlin College that "twenty-nine men decided for the Christian life, or renewed allegiance."[14] In 1906, during the second semester at Campbell College in Holton, Kansas, sixty students either "renewed their vows" or began the Christian life.[15] The "revival of very great power" which swept Trinity College in Durham, North Carolina, left no more than twenty-five unconverted students at the entire school, while at the University of Michigan two-thirds of the male students—2,400 men no less— came to University Hall to hear the proclamation of the gospel.[16]

A letter written to J.R. Mott during this general era by Henry Wright, a professor of Greek at Yale University, describes the religious awakening at Yale:

> I can't help thinking what a lot it will mean for the Church of Christ to have 500 men graduate from Yale this year who not only have heard, but who know by experience that a religious

awakening among educated men is not only possible but, more than that, necessary....Not a night has passed but some man has come in to tell me of a new man who took a stand in the meetings or who has made things right with the folks at home. The real number who have come out for Christ is nearer 100 than eighty-eight.[17]

One visible fruit of the awakening was the monumental increase in student Bible study groups, particularly among the collegiate YMCA. The University of Florida found this to be true as every campus fraternity organized Bible study meetings for their respective members. At Vanderbilt in Tennessee, the captain, manager and a host of other players from the football team routinely assembled to strengthen both body and soul in a "football Bible class." And at Tuskegee Institute in Alabama, enrollment in Bible classes grew from twenty to one hundred and twenty within the span of one short year![18]

Interest in noon meetings for prayer at the Massachusetts Institute of Technology tripled in 1906 with the seven fraternity classes that had been organized earlier in the year "proving successful" in this regard.[19] Two Kansas colleges saw a remarkable increase in Bible study enrollment, "from twelve and fifteen respectively to seventy-five and eighty."[20] A sister institution, Kansas State Agriculture College, boasted of twenty-nine Bible study groups whose registration totalled 380 men.[21] The YMCA at Drake University, in Iowa, saw participation triple as compared to previous years.[22] The growth of the World Student Christian Federation was likewise affected: membership skyrocketed from the original 11,725 participants to 103,000, with registered Student Christian Societies expanding from 301 to 925![23]

There was also an increased burden for the lost and an unprecedented increase in missionary interest. Prior to 1895, for example, less than 1,000 student volunteers were on the mission field. In May 1906, a record 3,500 student missionaries sailed from either America or Europe to foreign ports as missionaries.[24] The fifth quadrennial gathering of the National Convention of Student Volunteers reported delegates to have increased six-fold in less than fifteen years, with the 1905 registrants totalling over 4,000![25] Veteran missionary and distinguished historian K.S. Latourette (1884–1968), an alumnus of Yale, suggested that out of the class that enrolled as freshmen in 1905 "came more missionaries than from any other class in the history of Yale College."[26]

Along with the YMCA, the Student Volunteer Movement for Foreign Missions and the World Student Christian Federation, additional student associations around the globe were also established or strengthened during this period of time, among them the European InterVarsity Fellowship. In 1935, this evangelical group invited Martyn Lloyd-Jones,[27] a man burdened for revival, to speak at their annual convention. In 1939 he played a "prominent part" at an event convened by IVF known as the International Conference of Evangelical Students. Later that same year, Lloyd-Jones agreed to serve as the president of the InterVarsity Fellowship.[28]

The expansion

To assist in the upsurge of spiritual growth within the collegiate community, the office of campus chaplain greatly expanded in various schools across the United States. To suggest that the chaplain's profession was new to this century would be inaccurate, as Yale College, for instance, appointed Naphtali Draggett to such a position in 1755.[29] Over the next century and a half, however, relatively few colleges followed Yale's precedent. There is good evidence that the rise in the number of paid chaplain positions in both church-related as well as state colleges in the early twentieth century was primarily due to the need felt by Evangelicals to find a way to counter to the growing secularization of the university community.[30] Be this as it may, it is quite evident that during the first decade of the twentieth century more workers than at any other previous time in history were led to organize Christian programs within the collegiate setting through the office most commonly known as campus chaplain.

Illustrations of this fact are numerous. For example, the Baptist State Associations of Michigan and Wisconsin championed this cause early in the century by securing funding for full-time chaplains to work with their state university students. It was the Wesley Guild that provided for a pastorate to serve the University at Ann Arbor, Michigan, in 1905. The Lutherans appointed Howard Gold to serve students at the University of Wisconsin, where he continued a solid work for nine years. The Presbyterians developed chaplaincy positions at universities located in Illinois, Kansas, Wisconsin, Colorado, Arkansas and Nebraska between 1905 and 1909. The Congregationalists were on board in 1906 when they called Richard Edwards to serve on the campus of the University of Wisconsin. Other denominations and schools were quick to follow suit.[31]

The global intensity of the 1904–1905 Welsh Revival lessened as the initial decade of the twentieth century came to a close and the onslaught of World War I unfolded. After that horrific war, various isolated outpourings of the Holy Spirit, however, still occurred on university campuses across the nation. The spring 1930 awakening at Eastern Nazarene College in Massachusetts illustrates this. J. Cameron, in writing on the history of this institution, describes the awakening in these words:

> The Holy Spirit broke in upon the campus without any human planning. No special services had been scheduled and no evangelist had been called. In fact there was very little preaching done during this revival. No classes were held for days as classrooms were turned into prayer rooms. At mealtime the dining room was often nearly empty as the students prayed and fasted.[32]

Wheaton College in Illinois, a school with a history of spiritual awakenings, also knew campus revival in 1936 and again in 1943. A participant in the 1936 event tells of his experience:

I went to chapel today, expecting only the usual kind of service: we got a real revival. Chapel began at about ten minutes
to ten, and did not let out until about twenty minutes after
eight in the evening. All the rest of the morning and all afternoon, the students were on their faces before God confessing
sin, and getting right with God. Many leaders confessed sin.
The Holy Spirit of God was truly here in real convicting
power. Many souls were saved today, too. At about eleven-
thirty, chapel was dismissed, but the Spirit overruled, and
classes were abandoned for the rest of the day.[33]

The 1943 revival at Wheaton deeply touched the President of
the Student Council, William ("Billy") Franklin Graham (1918–),
as well two other graduates, Torrey M. Johnson (1909–) and
Robert A. Cook, who went from the academic halls of Wheaton to
the streets of Chicago to develop a work known as Chicagoland
Youth For Christ. The initial target audience for this newly
formed organization, whose influence was later to also include the
college campus, was high school teens. As the Chicagoland Youth
For Christ expanded in scope across the nation, its name was
changed to Youth For Christ, with Billy Graham serving as the
leading YFC evangelist.[34]

Columbia Bible College similarly experienced revival in the
spring of 1936 following a brief visit by guest evangelist, J. Edwin
Orr. Robert C. McQuilken, who was then president of Columbia,
reported that "the regular weekly prayer meeting adjourned to a
larger hall at eight where over 400 crowded to hear the message.
The message was followed by confessions and prayers that lasted
until midnight."[35] Schools from coast to coast joined Wheaton and
Columbia throughout 1936 in a series of collegiate awakenings
that "included unusual prayer, a great expectancy, faithful preaching, a personal challenge, deep conviction, a thorough confession,
immediate restitution, certain forgiveness, contagious joy, happy
testimony, renewed power and tender concern for others."[36]

Sadly, reports of campus revivals after 1936, with a few exceptions, dwindled almost entirely for about a dozen years. Throughout these years the YMCA, which historically had strongly promoted collegiate evangelistic activities, missions and sound biblical study, was also gradually changing its areas of primary focus. Diminishing interest in the salvation, training and sending out of college students was a fruit of such change. The result was a massive plummet in the attendance at YMCA Bible studies. Enrollment fell by over 25,000 registered college students during the 1920s alone![37] The Student Volunteer Movement likewise decreased significantly in both scope and power during this general era. This is not to suggest, however, that chaplains and student workers were not persisting in Christian labour. In various colleges and universities, campus ministers continued in faithful service. Yet for those whose hearts knew what the God of history had accomplished in times past, surely their souls called heavenward for God to again drench the academic soil with the rains of revival. Their prayers were heard, and in the 1950s God again walked among students.

For reflection

As the early twentieth century revival began in Wales, Evan Roberts developed what one author suggested was "the revival's confession of faith." The following four articles were among the central emphases in the Welsh meetings.

> a) A confession to God of all sins of the past hitherto unconfessed.
> b) The giving up of everything doubtful.
> c) Open confession of Christ.
> d) Ready and immediate obedience to every impulse of the Spirit.[38]

1. If you were present in a 1904–1905 Welsh revival meeting where these emphases were being made, which of them do you believe the convicting hand of the Holy Spirit would tell you to pay close attention to? How will you answer his prompting?

2. A sad development throughout decades following this revival can be found in the histories of various universities and Christian organizations who, although conceived with a strong commitment to Christian orthodoxy, traded this commitment and allegiance to Jesus Christ for a theologically liberal agenda. Such was the experience of the YMCA, as other priorities took prominence over sound scriptural teaching, evangelism and missions. A loss of 25,000 Bible study registrants in one decade was the lamentable outcome! Many once-strong Christian colleges and universities likewise experienced spiritual deterioration as secularization was embraced over faith. Describe what you think a Christian campus student organization would be like if it confessed total allegiance to the Scriptures and practiced unrestricted obedience to the lordship of Jesus Christ. How does your fellowship compare? Based upon your present trends, what might your group be like in ten years?

For further study

As has been shown repeatedly throughout this book, revival occurs when the manifest presence of a holy God comes among a people, or a community, or a campus, or a nation. In essence, revival is not a program, but, as Martyn Lloyd-Jones is about to testify, the very "presence of God's Spirit among us." The following address, delivered in 1959 by Lloyd-Jones, is based upon the prayer found in Isaiah 64:1, a prayer in which the Prophet appeals to his sovereign God, boldly entreating him to "rend the heavens" and "come down!" Read the sermon and answer the following questions:

a) What is true prayer?

b) For what should we pray and why?

c) How should we pray?

d) Why should we read church history?

e) What personal challenge does this sermon pose to you?

D. Martyn Lloyd-Jones

David Martyn Lloyd-Jones (1899–1981) was born in Wales and moved with his family at the age of thirteen to London, England. It was in London that he trained for a career in medicine, and was on the verge of what promised to be a highly successful career when conversion to Christ led him to abandon his medical career for pastoral ministry. His first ministry was the Bethlehem Forward Movement Hall, a Calvinistic Methodist work at Sandfields, Aberavon. He served this church for over a decade. In 1938 G. Campbell Morgan (1863–1945), pastor of Westminster Chapel, London, asked Lloyd-Jones to join his staff as the associate pastor of this historic church. The offer was accepted, and when Morgan retired five years later it was Lloyd-Jones who was called to fill the pulpit. For a quarter of a century Lloyd-Jones served as pastor of Westminister Chapel, where his profoundly biblical teaching attracted a wide hearing. There is little doubt that his preaching ministry was one of the most influential ministries of the twentieth century.

Resources

For an excellent introduction to his life and the impact of his ministry, see the collection of essays edited by his grandson, Christopher Catherwood, *Martyn Lloyd-Jones: Chosen By God* (Illinois: Crossway Books, 1986). And in-depth study of his life can be found in the two-volume biography by Iain H. Murray: *David Martyn Lloyd-Jones. The First Forty Years 1899–1939* (Edinburgh: The Banner of Truth Trust, 1982) and *David Martyn Lloyd-Jones. The Fight of Faith 1939–1981* (Edinburgh: The Banner of Truth Trust, 1990). To obtain audio sermons, see "MLJ Recordings Trust" at www.mlj.org.uk. Also see "Dr Martyn Lloyd-Jones Online" at fly.hiwaay.net/~bsrich/mlj.htm.

Portrait of Martyn Lloyd-Jones by Desmond Groves (c.1970s).

A sermon by Martyn Lloyd-Jones:
Revival: The Presence of God's Spirit Among Us[39]

> Oh that thou wouldest rend the heavens, that thou wouldest
> come down, that the mountains might flow down at thy
> presence (Isaiah 64:1, KJV).

This man knew how to pray and did not need instruction about
prayer. Prayer is not easy; prayer, because we are what we are, is
difficult and we need instruction. If we have never felt what our
Lord's disciples felt when they turned to him one afternoon and
said "Lord, teach us how to pray," it is probably because we have
never really prayed at all. So God in his kindness has provided well
for us, with great patterns and examples and illustrations and we
have seen that the prophet looks back at them. He sees how God
has dealt with his people in the past, and then, having done that,
he beseeches him to look down upon them now, to behold their
condition, and to take again the interest that he once took in them.
He has a desire to see the face of God again, to know that he is well
disposed towards them and to feel that he is taking a loving interest in them.

But he does not stop at that, and true prayer through the ages
has never stopped at that; it can never be satisfied with that alone.
There is always this further petition which is contained in this
sixty-fourth chapter. Here again we find that there is really only
one prayer, but it has all the characteristics which true praying
always has. You notice the first word "Oh." I would remind you
again that true praying is always characterized by the use of that
word, "Oh"—"Oh that thou wouldest rend the heavens." There is
no word that is more expressive of longing than that word. It
expresses the thirst of deep desire, it is the cry of a man at the end
of his resources and waiting and looking for, and longing for God.

That is one obvious characteristic, but we also find here, as we
have already seen, the alternation of petition and confession, the

claims that are made, and all the arguments and disputations with God. These are always the characteristics of true praying. In other words this man is really, as he puts it himself, laying hold upon God. He is lifting himself up to pray, and he is taking hold of God. It is an extraordinary expression and yet how true it is. That is true prayer—not a mere casual expression of our desire, not something perfunctory and half-hearted. Real prayer means taking hold of God and not letting go. You will find it all in the famous instance of Jacob, struggling with the "man" who appeared to him on that critical night before he had to meet his brother Esau. Jacob struggled with him, he wrestled with him and when the day broke and the man said that he must go, Jacob said, "I will not let thee go, except thou bless me" (Genesis 32:26). Taking hold of God, laying hold upon him, pleading with him, reasoning, and even beseeching, and I say that it is only when the Christian arrives at that position that he truly begins to pray.

So we have here his final great petition—"Oh that thou wouldest rend the heavens, that thou wouldest come down"—and I do not hesitate to assert that is the ultimate prayer in connection with a revival. It is right, of course, always to pray to God to bless us, to look upon us and to be gracious unto us, that should be our constant prayer. But this goes beyond that, and it is here that we see the difference between what the church should always be praying for, and the special, peculiar, urgent prayer for a visitation of God's Spirit in revival. There is no term that better expresses this ultimate petition than does that phrase in [William] Cowper's hymn:

Oh rend the heavens, come quickly down,
And make a thousand hearts thine own.

We do not often see a thousand hearts turning to God in Christ, do we? But that is what happens in revival. Cowper has got the right petition—"rend the heavens"—and when God rends the heavens we may well see a thousand, or three thousand as on the day of Pentecost—"Make a thousand hearts thine own." This is a prayer for something unusual, something quite exceptional and it is at the same time a reminder to us of what revival really is, there is no better way of putting it than this. It is indeed God's coming down, God, as it were, no longer merely granting us the blessings. We have to use such terms, and yet, in a sense, they are very foolish. Everything that God does is marvellous and wonderful and transcends our highest imagination and yet we find these contrasts in the Scriptures between God doing what he normally does, and God doing the unusual, God coming down.

And, always, of course, accompanying this is the thing which the prophet in particular emphasizes here: it is also a manifestation of the power of God, not only the glory and the radiance of God's presence—but especially his power—notice the terms which he uses—"Oh," he says, "that thou wouldest *rend* the heavens." There is a tearing process, God erupts into the midst. We are told that he has come down, "that the mountains might flow down at thy presence," these great mountains that seem everlasting and eternal, that are always there whether the wind blows or not, whether the rain comes or is withheld, whether the sun shines or is clouded over. These are the everlasting hills and mountains, but when God comes down even the mountains begin to flow.

This, then, is the power that we, too, should realize and should pray for. Indeed, half our troubles in our praying are due to the fact that we fail to realize the greatness and the power of God. We are troubled about the enemies of the church, we see the arrogance and the power of the world, but there is a prophecy which will be fulfilled one day. "But the day of the Lord will come as a thief in the night; in the which the heavens shall pass away with a great noise, and the elements shall melt with fervent heat, the earth also and the works that are therein shall be burned up" (2 Peter 3:10). That day is coming, let there be no mistake about this, that is the power of God. This solid universe, these everlasting hills, the elements, they are all going to melt away, all will be dissolved and disrupted. The heavens themselves will pass away, heaven and earth will pass away. So we must remind ourselves to whom we pray. He is a God of great power. "Oh that thou wouldest rend the heavens, that thou wouldest come down, that the mountains might flow down at thy presence." That is the power of God and we must never lose sight of that.

The Apostle Paul, too, puts it in his way. There were troubles in the church at Corinth and the Apostle writes to them, "For the weapons of our warfare *are* not carnal, but mighty through God to the pulling down of strong holds; Casting down imaginations, and every high thing that exalteth itself against the knowledge of God, and bringing into captivity every thought to the obedience of Christ" (2 Corinthians 10:4–5). Are we clear about this power of God? Are we clear about its illimitable character? Do we modern Christians realize that "the weapons of our warfare are not carnal, but mighty through God to the pulling down of strongholds"? Are you troubled still about all these philosophies and ideologies and politics, and everything that is opposed to God, the anti-God movements? Why all this talk about the enemy? Have we forgotten about the power of God? Our God is a God who can rend the very heavens, and cause the mountains to flow and the sea to boil, as if it were but water in a kettle. The everlasting God. The power of God—that is what the prophet prays for. He prays that the glory and the power of God may be made manifest. Are we praying that prayer? Is that our innermost desire? Are we at all concerned about the present situation? Why should Isaiah pray like this? And why should we not pray in the same way? Why should praying like this be confined to certain people now and again in the long history of the church? Why does every Christian not feel this?

Now that is the question, so let me put it positively, why should we pray like this? Let that now be our second consideration. The prophet answers that question. He has a reason, these men of God always have a reason for praying, and you and I must, too, have reasons or we shall never pray. The prophet is praying that God may come down as when the melting fire burns and causes the waters to boil (Isaiah 64:2), and the reason for this prayer is—"To make thy name known to thine adversaries." That is the first reason, and you notice that in the Bible, it is always the first reason. These men prayed to God as they did, because they had a zeal for the name and the glory of God. Come down, he says, that these adversaries of thine may know thy name. You notice that he says that they are God's adversaries. Why does he not say that they are our adversaries? That would have been true, yes, but he has a deeper insight than that, and that is where we go wrong so frequently. We will persist in regarding the church as a human institution, we are fighting for our lives, trying to keep the doors open, trying to keep the church going, so we put up our commissions and we multiply our organizations—our adversaries, that is what we are fighting. No, says the prophet, they are God's adversaries.

This is a great theme in the Old Testament and in the New. In Psalm 99 the Psalmist says, "The Lord reigneth; let the people tremble: he sitteth *between* the cherubims; let the earth be moved." The Lord reigneth. Let the people tremble, for he is the living God, the everlasting God, the God in whose hand all things are. Oh, the tragedy of a world that does not know him, oh, the arrogance and the pride of these nations and people and rulers who defy him.

In Revelation 6 we are told that at the manifestation of his glory kings and the great of the earth will cry out unto the rocks and unto the mountains, "Fall on us, and hide us...from the wrath of the Lamb." The Lord reigneth, let the nations tremble at thy presence. In Psalm 46 the Psalmist works it all out, and concludes with these great words "Be still, and know that I am God" (verse 10). You foolish people who are arguing against God—"He maketh wars to cease" (Psalm 46:9). Of course he does. He can do anything that he likes, there is nothing that he cannot do. He created everything out of nothing, he said, "Let there be light," and there was light. He is the eternal God, the Creator, the controller of the ends of the earth. "Be still, and know"—and admit—"that I am God." That is what this man is praying for. Oh God, he says, why do you not come down, that these adversaries of thine may know thy name, and tremble in thy presence? Christian people, I do not understand you if you are not offering this same prayer, as you see the arrogance of so-called learning and the impudence of all that claims to be cultural. As you see men and women, in their fineries, and in their rags, blaspheming the name of this Holy God, do you not feel like asking him to give just a part of his power to silence them and to cause them to tremble in his holy presence? That is what this man felt. That is what God's people have always felt when they have truly prayed for revival.

And then the last reason for his prayer is the one that Isaiah gives at the very end of the chapter—the state of God's realm. But he puts that last, you see. *We* start with it, of course, we are all so subjective and self-centred, we start with ourselves and we end with ourselves. Not this man, oh, this is the thing that is hurting him—those adversaries. Come down, he says, let them know thy name, let them be humbled before thee and finally:

> Be not wroth very sore, O Lord, neither remember iniquity for ever: behold, see, we beseech thee, we *are* all thy people. Thy holy cities are a wilderness, Zion is a wilderness, Jerusalem a desolation. Our holy and our beautiful house, where our fathers praised thee, is burned up with fire: and all our pleasant things are laid waste. Wilt thou refrain thyself for these things, O Lord? wilt thou hold thy peace, and afflict us very sore? (Isaiah 64:9–12, KJV).

Have mercy upon us, say those who pray for revival, and upon the state of thy church. Behold what we are and remember what we once were, think of thine own heritage, thine own church, make her again glorious. There, then, are the reasons for praying as the prophet did.

But let us now consider the encouragements that there are for us to pray like this. I shall just give you some headings, and you can work them out for yourselves. The first encouragement to such prayer is what God has done in the past. In verse 3 Isaiah says, "When thou didst terrible things *which* we looked not for, thou camest down, the mountains flowed down at thy presence." It is as if he were saying, "I am not asking the impossible, I am simply asking you to do what you have already done before." Let me repeat: the greatest tonic to a drooping spirit is to read the history of the church. Read the history of the church, my friends, it did not start when Moody first came to this country, it goes back through the running centuries; go back, read the story and consider what God has done in ages past. There is nothing so stimulating to prayer as that, and you notice the interesting way in which he puts it: "When thou didst terrible things which we looked not for." "You know," says this man, in effect, in his prayer, "In the past, Oh God, you surprised your own people. You did things that they would never have imagined." He did it of course in Egypt, where they were in an impossible situation; slaves in the hands of powerful Pharaoh and his hosts, and his chariots. They had not a sword, they had nothing. Taskmasters laid their lashes upon the backs of the poor people; what hope was there for them? But out they came—God led them out. "Thou didst strange things, terrible things which we looked not for." Pharaoh did not want to let them go, but God soon made him.

And then there they were, facing the Red Sea with the hosts of Pharaoh behind them. Impossible? Not at all. God divided the sea. This is the God whom we are worshipping and to whom we are praying, when we see these things "which we looked not for." And again, in the desert, there they were, in a howling, barren wilderness, with nothing to eat; and God provided them with bread from heaven. Then there was no water, and it seemed they would die of thirst. At God's command Moses struck the rock and out came the gushing water; "things that we looked not for." That is our God, my friends.

And you and I have even greater encouragements than those which this prophet Isaiah had. The greatest thing happened when the fullness of the times had come and God sent forth his Son, made of a woman, made under the Law. Shall God verily dwell with man? He has done. God rent the heavens and sent forth his

Son, and the Son came out of the clouds of glory and entered the Virgin's womb. Things that we thought not of, things that we had never looked for. God has done them. Ah yes, you say, but Jesus of Nazareth was defeated by his enemies, he was taken and condemned and killed. He died, they buried him in a grave, there is the end. No, he burst asunder, he rent asunder (the same word) the bands of death, and he rose triumphant o'er the grave. The resurrection is behind us. He is the God of the resurrection, death is conquered, the grave has lost its power. "O death, where *is* thy sting? O grave, where *is* thy victory?" (2 Corinthians 15:55)

But, you may say, that does not help us very much because he has gone back to heaven and left just these twelve ordinary, ignorant men, these disciples, these apostles so-called. As these twelve men and some companions of theirs, were meeting together in an upper room at the Feast of Pentecost, suddenly there was a sound from heaven as of a mighty rushing wind. What has happened? Oh, God has rent the heavens and has come down. It is the descent of the Holy Ghost. The sound of a mighty rushing wind filling the house. God rending the heavens. We can look back on that. Let us remind God of it, he is the same God. He sent the Holy Spirit, he has sent him since. Go back and read the story of the Protestant Reformation, read of the mighty revival of two hundred years ago affecting London and the provinces and other countries. Go back and read again the story of 1859. What are all these? Rent heavens! God rending the heavens and coming down, coming among his people, displaying his power and his glory. "The sound of a rushing mighty wind." "When thou didst terrible things which we looked not for." The encouragement of history is a great encouragement, is it not?

And then let me encourage you with the promises of God. What a glorious word we find in verse 5: "Thou meetest him that rejoiceth and worketh righteousness, *those that* remember thee, in thy ways." Thank God for this. How do I know that God is going to listen to me and to give me my petition? Here is the answer—he is ready to meet certain people—"Thou meetest." He has promised to do this. Who does he meet? He meets with those who work right-eousness and who rejoice in doing so. He meets with all, as the end of verse 4 has told us, who wait for him. Have no doubt about that, my dear friends. Listen to James as he says, "Draw nigh to God, and he will draw nigh to you" (James 4:8). It is a fact, it is certain, he meets such people. If, with all your heart ye truly seek him, ye shall surely find him. Have you sought him? Have you found him? He has promised it. Draw near unto God and he will draw near unto you. "Thou meetest...those that remember thee in thy ways." Of course he does. Blessed be his name.

Oh what blessed encouragements to pray. The character of God, not only his might and his power and his glory, but his compassion, his loving kindness, his tender mercy, yes, grace abounding to the vilest of sinners. While we were yet dead in sins, while we were enemies, we were reconciled to God by the death of his Son. "God commended his love towards us, in that, while we were yet sinners, Christ died for us" (Romans 5:8).

God's displeasure is upon the church because of her sin, because of her apostasy and her rebellion, but if she truly repents and really seeks him, he will yet meet with her. "Thou shalt find him, if thou seek him with all thy heart." (Deuteronomy 4:29).

Seek him, stir yourself up to call upon his name. Take hold upon him, plead with him as your Father, as your Maker, as your Potter, as your Guide, as your God. Plead his own promises. Cry unto him and say, "Oh that thou wouldest rend the heavens, that thou wouldest come down."

Oh rend the heavens, come quickly down,
And make a thousand hearts thine own.
—William Cowper

1   On this revival, see especially Eifion Evans, *The Welsh Revival of 1904* (3rd ed.; Bryntirion, Bridgend: Evangelical Press of Wales, 1987).

2   J. Edwin Orr, *The Flaming Tongue* (Chicago: Moody Press, 1973), 66–67.

3   J. Edwin Orr, *The Light of the Nations* (Grand Rapids: Wm. B. Eerdmans Publishing Co., 1965), 235.

4   Clarence P. Shedd, *Two Centuries of Student Christian Movements* (New York: Association Press, 1934), 375–376.

5   Clarence P. Shedd, *The Church Follows Its Students* (New York: Yale University Press, 1938), 9.

6   Orr, *Light of the Nations*, 230–231.

7   Orr, *Flaming Tongue*, 16.

8   J. Edwin Orr, *Campus Aflame* (Glendale, California: Regal Books, 1971), 102.

9   Orr, *Flaming Tongue*, 72.

10   *Missionary Review of the World* (July 1905), 524–525.

11   *The Intercollegian* 27 (March 1905), 144.

12   *The Intercollegian* 29 (April 1907), 157.

13   *The Intercollegian* 27 (May 1905), 188.

14   *The Intercollegian* 28 (June 1906), 228.

15   *The Intercollegian* 28 (April 1906), 176.

16   Orr, *Flaming Tongue*, 87–88.

17   Basil Mathews, *John R. Mott, World Citizen* (New York: Wm. B. Eerdmans, 1934), 156–157.

18   *The Intercollegian* 28 (April 1906), 176.

19   *The Intercollegian* 28 (May 1906), 199.

20   *The Intercollegian* 28 (March 1906), 149.

21   *The Intercollegian* 28 (April 1906), 176.

22   *The Intercollegian* 27 (February 1905), 135.

23   *Missionary Review of the World*, (July 1905), 524–525.

24   *Missionary Review of the World*, (May 1906), 370.

25   *Missionary Review of the World*, (May 1906), 370.

26   *Beyond the Ranges* (Grand Rapids, Michigan: Wm. B. Eerdmans, 1967), 35.

27   For a message from this distinguished twentieth-century preacher entitled *Revival: the Presence of God's Spirit Among Us*, see the conclusion of the chapter.

28   Iain H. Murray *David Martyn Lloyd-Jones, The First Forty Years 1899–1939* (Edinburgh: The Banner of Truth Trust, 1982), 297, 374.

29   S.A. Smith, *The American College Chaplaincy* (New York: Association Press, 1954), 4.

30   Orr, *Flaming Tongue*, 90.

31   Shedd, *Church Follows Its Students*, 16–35.

32   J. Cameron, *Eastern Nazarene College* (Kansas City, Missouri: Nazarene Publishing House, 1968), 201.

33 J.E. Orr, *This is the Victory* (Grand Rapids: Zondervan Publishing House, 1936), 37.

34 Mel Larson, *Young Man on Fire: The Story of Torrey Johnson and Youth For Christ* (Chicago: Youth Publications, 1945), 79–93.

35 A.J. Appasamy, *Write the Vision* (Port Washington, Pennsylvania: Christian Literature Crusade, 1964), 147.

36 Appasamy, *Write the Vision*, 148.

37 C. Howard Hopkins, *History of the Y.M.C.A. in North America* (New York: Association Press, 1951), 644–645.

38 H. Elvet Lewis, G. Campbell Morgan, and I.V. Neprash, *Glory Filled the Land: A Trilogy on the Welsh Revival, 1904–1905*, ed. Richard Owen Roberts (Wheaton, Illinois: International Awakening Press, 1989), 44–45.

39 From *Revival* by Martyn Lloyd-Jones, copyright ©1987, pp.304–316. Used by permission of Crossway Books, a division of Good News Publishers, Wheaton, Illinois 60187. This sermon has been edited for this book.

5

"God moved into our midst"

Mid to late twentieth century campus revivals

The setting

For the Christian community in the United States, the decades preceding the mid-century resurgence can perhaps best be described as a time of transition, redefinition and rebuilding. Many evangelical students and chaplains, for example, who had previously affiliated with the YMCA, found it necessary to develop a variety of new organized campus groups, the largest of which was known as the League of Evangelical Students (LES).[1] For various reasons, the LES also declined in effectiveness throughout the late 1930s and early 1940s, the same time in which God was advancing yet another student group known as InterVarsity Christian Fellowship (IVCF). Youth For Christ (YFC), as was noted in the previous chapter, was likewise established during this period, as was the Navigators.

In response to the progressive collapse of the Student Volunteer Movement, a number of students were inspired to develop an organization entitled the Student Foreign Missions Fellowship (SFMF).[2] Yet another transition occurred when the SFMF joined forces with IVCF to further advance the cause of global missions within the collegiate community. The Urbana Missions Conference was a fruit of their union, a triennial gathering that to this day remains the largest student missions conference of its kind in the world.[3] However, despite all the beneficial initiation and rebuilding of evangelical collegiate organizations, the years between the two World Wars were sadly marked by a general "lack of nationwide revivals."[4]

Many denominational colleges were likewise caught in the winds of change and redefinition. Some became completely secular institutions and forgot the godly heritage established by their founding fathers. Other schools took extreme positions on the theological spectrum. Some stressed what became known as Fundamentalism, in which matters of cultural preference were given as prominent a place as Christian orthodoxy. Others favoured what is known as the Social Gospel, in which Christian ethics and the activity of building the Kingdom of God took priority over doctrine.[5]

In fact, it was not just the Christian community, but in fact the entire country, which had earlier struggled through the Great Depression only to find itself thrust into the horror of the Second World War, that was caught in an era of transition, redefinition and rebuilding. It was into this changing climate, approaching the 1950s, that the Spirit of God issued the call to revival.

The awakening

The collegiate awakening of the 1950s did not occur, as some have argued, at Wheaton College in Illinois, at Asbury in Kentucky or even with the 600 students of Bethel College in Minnesota. Quite the contrary, its genesis was in a small office in Minneapolis, late at night in April of 1949, where four men found themselves compelled to pray for revival. Two of the four, William Dunlap and Jack Frank, were students from Los Angeles, California. They had been so deeply burdened for a student awakening through previous contacts with J. Edwin Orr that they drove 2,300 miles to join Orr and another young evangelist, none other than Billy Graham, for a season of passionate prayer.[6] In May of that same year, Orr was invited by Bethel College to hold a series of meetings on revival. Orr's ministry resulted in an awakening on the Bethel campus.[7] This is the way that one writer describes the scene at Bethel:

The preaching in Bethel Chapel became very strong. There was much prayer in the dormitories, followed by intense conviction of sin among the students in chapel and in classroom. Conviction was relieved only by outright confession, restitution, restoration or conversion to God....At the height of the conviction, when hundreds of students wanted to confess failure or ask for prayer or testify of deliverance, the full chapel service was broken up into a dozen smaller meetings...[8]

It was early in 1950 that a revival also occurred at Wheaton College. It was one that had more far-reaching ramifications than any preceding awakening on the campus.[9] In describing this awakening, *Time* magazine reported that "all night long, all the next day, all through the following night, and half of the following day, students poured out confessions of past sins and rededicated themselves to God."[10]

A few weeks later the students at Asbury in Kentucky experienced a similar Pentecost. W. Holland, who was then a professor at Asbury, recalls:

So mighty was the presence of the Holy Spirit in that chapel service that the students could not refrain from testimony. The guest speaker had little opportunity for his message. The floodgates of heaven lifted and God moved into our midst as I have never before witnessed....Testimonies were followed by confessions, confessions by crowded altars, crowded altars gave place to glorious spiritual victories, and this in turn to more testimonies. Thus, it ran for several days.... At times the Divine Presence was so pronounced that one could gather some conception of what Saint Paul must have experienced when he was caught up into the Third Heaven.[11]

At John Brown University in Arkansas there was also a revival that "appeared to be entirely spontaneous" with "scores of students" embracing eternal life. A similar work of the Spirit at California

Seminary brought such conviction that some students were, for over four hours, unable to move from their knees! The pupils at Whitworth College in Spokane, Washington petitioned the administration to invite an evangelist for a series of meetings early in 1950. The fruit of their efforts was seen in "a time of genuine revival and spiritual deepening in the whole student body." A Campus Christian Crusade, led by William Bright (1921–) on the University of California at Los Angeles, had 150 professions of faith in Christ. Bright and his colleagues were encouraged to extend their ministry to other campuses and Campus Crusade for Christ was born![12]

Expansion

Stanley Rowland, in an article written for an October 1955 edition of *The New York Times*, noted the ongoing work of God's Spirit within the collegiate community. According to his findings "more than 1,200 of the nation's 1,900 colleges and universities now have a "religious emphasis week of some sort," with interest doubling from previous years.[13]

This growth in spiritual interest was partly the result of Inter-Varsity Christian Fellowship. Throughout the winter/spring semester of 1951, for instance, numerous evangelists, including J. Edwin Orr, visited approximately sixty-five IVCF campuses from Maine to California. Although these meetings did not actually issue in revival, there were records of rebirth at nearly every one of the recorded "missions," as they were called.[14] Throughout the next four decades, IVCF expanded its student-led chapters and related ministries with a diversity of evangelism, discipleship and missions programing. During this same period, IVCF field staff enlarged from 50 to 476, with over 23,000 students registering involvement during the 1989–1990 academic year! And today there are more than 1,000 InterVarsity staff serving more than 34,000 students and faculty nationwide.[15]

Campus Crusade for Christ was likewise involved in augmenting the work of Christ during this era of spiritual expansion. By

1960, Campus Crusade had grown from its humble genesis on the University of California at Los Angeles to a presence on over forty campuses in fifteen states with staff numbering in excess of 100. Currently Campus Crusade for Christ is present on 1,255 campuses worldwide, with 1,310 campus ministry staff working alongside an additional 4,227 volunteer staff. Crusade personnel minister around the globe through multimedia, campus and city-wide crusades, athletics, music, conferences, publishing and a variety of other ministry channels.[16] The 1950s also saw a host of trained volunteers entering college communities as returning World War II servicemen. Many who had involved themselves in Navigator-based Bible studies and witnessing instruction, went back to the academic world. Interestingly, the Navigators' headquarters encouraged the veterans not to start separate Navigator groups on their respective campuses, but to work alongside InterVarsity, and later Campus Crusade, and other existing evangelical collegiate associations in winning and discipling students for Christ. In the decade of the 1960s, the Navigators continued many of their co-operative relationships as well as reaffirmed their uniqueness through the development of their own particular campus ministry programs. Today, the Navigators are ministering on over 150 college campuses through their full-time staff and volunteer leadership.[17]

A growing interest among students in missionary service followed this mid-century awakening in ways reminiscent of the Student Volunteer Movement for Foreign Missions in the early years of the twentieth century. An illustration of this growth of interest in missions can be found in the 1946 conference entitled the International Missionary Convention, later known as Urbana, which grew steadily from 576 students at its first event to over 17,000 nearly a half-century later! The expansion during the first decade alone was sixfold.[18] Many military veterans, through their exposure in military service to global need, found themselves drawn to missions. Groups such as the Missionary Aviation Fellowship, Eastern Gospel Crusade and Greater European Mission were primarily initiated by such veterans.[19]

The Asbury awakening and the spring 1995 visitation

Similar to a number of the awakenings we have looked at in this book, Asbury College experienced revival in 1970. What began as a routine morning chapel service on February 3 that year, continued uninterruptedly for 185 hours! Two days later Taylor University in Upland, Indiana, had a similar experience. One participant/observer described it as nothing short of a "tremendous outpouring" of the Holy Spirit.

The awakening at Asbury sent out a torrent of revived students to colleges, seminaries and churches throughout twenty states and to Canada. Through Asbury student testimonies, the Christian community at Greenville College in Illinois, for example, experienced "night-and-day-long scenes of prayer, praise, waiting, witnessing, singing and exhortation." Houghton College was likewise visited by a group whom the Holy Spirit used to spark "testimonies, confession and prayer" lasting late into the night.[20] Henry C. James, the Director of Publicity at Asbury during this season of grace, suggested that by the summer of 1970 no less than 130 colleges, seminaries and Bible schools had been touched by the Spirit of revival![21]

It was a quarter of a century since the Asbury awakening when God once again powerfully walked on campus. In the spring of 1995, God's footprints were again visible on the collegiate soil of approximately forty schools.

Most would agree that the genesis of this recent work of grace was on Sunday morning, January 22, 1995, at the Coggin Avenue Baptist Church in Brownwood, Texas. Chris Robeson, a student from nearby Howard Payne University, was present in the church that morning. During the course of the service, he felt impelled to meditate on Joel 2:12–13. Intense self-examination followed, and by the conclusion of the worship hour, he went to the pulpit to publicly share his personal convictions. The Spirit used his testimony throughout the congregation to bring "brokenness for about an hour and a half." When the prolonged service had concluded, no less than twenty-two persons had either found the Saviour or embraced a call to ministry![22]

The believers on the campus of Howard Payne University caught wind of God's work within their community, meetings on campus were held and the fire of revival spread. Seven hundred students were reportedly at the largest gathering, with hundreds visibly impacted. Beason Divinity School was likewise impacted, as were Eastern Kentucky University, Kentucky State, Wayland Baptist University, Houston Baptist University and Southwestern Baptist Seminary.[23] At Southwestern, a routine forty-five-minute chapel service turned into a twelve-hour meeting marked by a "deep conviction of sin" within many who were present.[24]

At Wheaton College, a Sunday evening service that hosted two Howard Payne students continued throughout the night. Brokenness and repentance were distinguishing features of the worship.[25] Similar meetings continued at Wheaton for five consecutive evenings, with approximately 250 students affirming a call to vocational Christian service.[26] Howard Payne students shared on various other campuses as well, including Gordon College and Eastern Baptist University, with similar impact.

As Wheaton students went and shared what God was doing at various other schools—including Trinity Evangelical Divinity School in Illinois, Ashland University in Ohio, Northwestern College in Iowa, Taylor University in Indiana, as well as the Michigan institutions of Cornerstone College and Grand Rapids Baptist Seminary—awakenings of various proportions was reported at each institution. The chaplain at Northwestern, for instance, said that the revival on their campus was nothing short of "a purifying flame,"[27] while the meetings at Cornerstone in Grand Rapids were characterized by a "true, deep, genuine spirit of repentance" as students "came to terms with the seriousness of sin."

Perhaps Ashland University was the last academic institution to be impacted during the spring of 1995. The author was present at this awakening and submitted an article describing the revival to a denominational magazine, *The Brethren Evangelist*. The following portion from that article, which detailed events seemingly common to most of the spring 1995 collegiate visitations, recalls memories that still elicit deep personal emotions of gratitude and joy:

> The evening was both peaceful and genuine, with every appearance that only the Holy Spirit of God was in charge. Some students wept at the pulpit with a brokenness of heart...others ran to their dorms to gather friends or to reconcile broken relationship. The recommitments to faith were too numerous to count. Clusters of students could be found around the chapel sharing tears, reconciliation, support, and prayer. The public testimonies and confessions began at 10:00 P.M. and continued without interruption for a full three-and-a-half hours. A witness to the genuineness of this movement of the Spirit was the fact that spontaneous meetings for prayer, praise, and confession of sin, accompanied by bold witnessing, continued from April 26th until the end of the semester.[28]

Just prior to the 1949–1950 awakening, the late Dr. J. Edwin Orr suggested that "the revival for which we pray has begun, but...it is developing by stages. To my mind, the next step will be the reviving of Christian students, in the theological seminaries and Christian colleges and secular universities. Christian students are among the leaders of the coming generation."[29] Might this statement also be a word for *our* time? Listen—do you hear the footsteps of God?

For reflection

1. When the mid-century revival engulfed Bethel College in May of 1949, hundreds of students experienced an intense and personal encounter with the Holy Spirit. The fruit of his work among the student body was, in part, evidenced by the restoration of broken relationships. If you were praying in the Chapel at Bethel College in May, 1949, would there be a broken or strained relationship evident in your life that the convicting hand of Holy Spirit might bring to mind? If he asked you to initiate the process of reconciliation with this particular individual, how would you respond?

2. When the Spirit of revival came to Asbury in 1950, W. Holland, then a professor at the College, recalled that the presence of the Holy Spirit in that chapel service was so powerful that "the students could not refrain from testimony." If you were asked to testify at a weekly meeting concerning the present work of the Holy Spirit in your life, what is it that you would share?

3. Shortly before the 1949–1950 awakening, J. Edwin Orr suggested that "the revival for which we pray has begun, but…it is developing by stages. To my mind, the next step will be the reviving of Christian students, in the theological seminaries and Christian colleges and secular universities." What do you believe should be a focus of concerted prayer for your particular campus?

For further study

Originally addressed by J. Edwin Orr to a college audience, the following message entitled The First Word of the Gospel[30] *illustrates the centrality of the doctrine of repentance throughout Scripture, as well the difference between genuine and fraudulent repentance. If Orr is in fact correct in his assertion that repentance is* The First Word of the Gospel, *then should not each earnest believer desire to know and practice the essential truths related to this vital doctrine? If such is your desire, then allow the following message by J. Edwin Orr to guide both your mind and heart.*

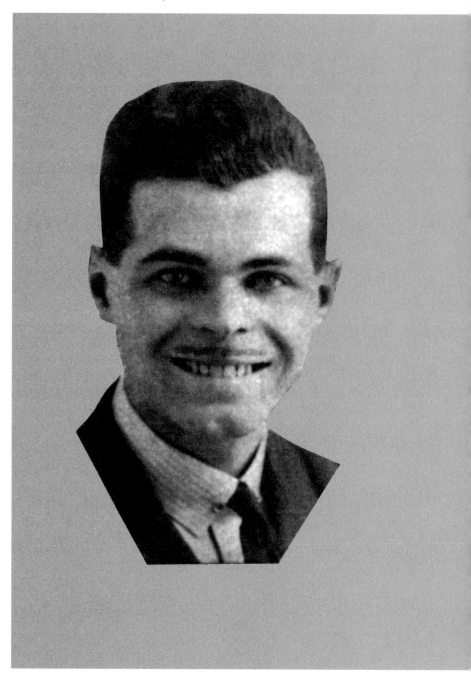

J. Edwin Orr

J. Edwin Orr (1912–1987) was a native of Belfast, Ireland. He was converted at the age of nine, and throughout much of his life served internationally as a prominent speaker on revival as well as a prolific writer on this subject. His professional career included pastoral ministry in Toronto, Ontario, Canada, chaplaincy service during the Second World War, and teaching at Fuller Theological Seminary. He had earned degrees in science, history and theology, including a D.Phil. from Oxford University. In his lifetime of evangelistic travels Orr visited all but ten of the world's countries, while visiting 400 of its 600 major cities! Collectively, his writings have sold in excess of one million copies.

Resources

For a brief review of his career, see the "Appendix: J. Edwin Orr (1912–1987): Historian of Revivals" by Michael A.G. Haykin on page 131. Orr wrote numerous books on revivals throughout the history of the church and around the world. His major work was *The Second Evangelical Awakening. An account of the Second Worldwide Evangelical Revival beginning in the Mid-Nineteenth Century* (Abridged ed.; London/Edinburgh: Marshall, Morgan & Scott, 1955). For the titles of Orr's other writings, see the citations in the footnotes of the Appendix.

Photo of J. Edwin Orr, from J. Edwin Orr, *Can God—?* (London: Marshall, Morgan & Scott, Ltd., 1935), cover.

A sermon by J. Edwin Orr:
The First Word of the Gospel

It goes without saying that a major concern of public health is what experts and laymen alike call "birth defects," the physical handicaps that afflict the unfortunates whose entrance into life was marred by some accident of nature, some deficiency of formation which cannot be blamed upon their progenitors.

Is it not also possible that many ills of the Christian life are due to handicapped beginnings in spiritual birth? That unfortunates, whose professed conversion was marred by a lack of understanding of what was involved, might find their spiritual life full of trials and woes not experienced by the children of God who were well born?

The news media made much of the announced conversion of a notorious pornographer whose journalism presented the public with smutty titillation which was not "naughty" but obscene. That he was "born-again" on his own say-so was accepted by the press, but perceptive Christians waited for evidence of a change of heart and lifestyle. None was forthcoming. His first editorial after the event told the world that he now followed the spirit of Jesus and Buddha.

There must be millions of professed Christians, much less notorious, who have suffered a bad beginning in the Christian life, whose profession of faith was much less open to blunt questioning by thinking people. It behooves us, therefore, to consider the initial experience of the Christian life before we can consider the living of it. What exactly is involved in becoming a Christian? What does it mean to be "born-again"? What does it mean to be converted?

It is interesting to notice the variety of responses when people are asked what is the first word of the good news of Jesus Christ? Some say only believe; others say love. Some say hope; others say heaven. And the odd person replies liberty, or civil rights. It was one man's protest that the gospel is so rich in its meaning that it is not possible to state a first word: it has many words of significance.

The alphabet has twenty-six letters, each of them useful but some much more used than others. But ask any kid in kindergarten:

"What is the first letter of the alphabet?" and he replies, "The letter A."
"And why is A the first letter of the alphabet?" And he says, "Because it is."
"But why do you say 'because it is'?" And the answer comes back with its devastating logic, "Because it comes first in the alphabet."

Which then, among the many words of the good news of Jesus Christ, is the first word? With which word does the gospel begin? The preliminary approaches of the Evangelists (as the discussion of water with the woman at the well) need not distract us. What is the first word of the message of the gospel?

If the first word in the mouth of John the Baptist was the first word in the mouth of the Lord Jesus, and if that was the first word in the mouth of the twelve disciples, and if that was the first word in the Lord's final instructions to his disciples, and if that was the first word of exhortation in the mouth of the Apostle Peter in his first great sermon at Pentecost, and if that was the first word in the mouth of the Apostle Paul throughout his ministry, surely that would be the first word!

So what was the first word in the mouth of John the Baptist? The third chapter of the Gospel of Matthew states it thus: "In those days came John the Baptist, preaching in the wilderness of Judea, 'Repent, for the kingdom of heaven is at hand.' " What was the first word in the message of our Lord? In the following chapter it is recorded: "From that time Jesus began to preach, saying: 'Repent, for the kingdom of heaven is at hand.' " Had the Lord Jesus preached before this? Apparently not. This then was his first message. And what was its first word? Unequivocally, it was the word *repent*. And the word occurs in verbal form three other times in the Gospel of Matthew, as part of the most compassionate of impassioned preaching of the Lord Jesus.

There are some who make a distinction between the good news of the kingdom of heaven and the good news of the kingdom of God. In the first chapter of the Gospel of Mark, it is recorded that after John the Baptist was put in prison Jesus himself came into Galilee, preaching the gospel of the kingdom of God, but the message was the same. After saying that "the time is fulfilled, the kingdom of God is at hand," the Lord said emphatically, "Repent and believe in the gospel." Also in Mark's Gospel, our Lord's calling and coaching of the twelve disciples is reported, after which "They went out and preached that men should repent."

Some may suggest that perhaps this first word *repent* gave way to some other exhortation as the ministry of the Lord and his disciples fully developed. The good news according to Luke, after mentioning the initial use of the word *repentance*, records it another ten times in verbal or substantive form, always in the preaching of the Lord Jesus, whether impassioned or compassionate. What is most significant is that in the last discourse of Jesus with the disciples, as recorded in the last chapter of Luke's Gospel, he stated plainly that the whole purpose of his death and resurrection was "that repentance and remission of sins should be preached in his name to all nations," beginning from Jerusalem. This constituted as certainly the Great Commission as did the command of Matthew 28.

It is fitting to ask whether the apostles who received the final commission were faithful in carrying it out. When the Apostle Peter reached the climax of his first great sermon at Pentecost, and his hearers cried out in conviction, "Men and brethren, what shall we do?," Peter recalled the parting instructions of his Lord, and told them to "Repent, and be baptized every one of you for the forgiveness of your sins," which was exactly what he and his companions had been told to declare. In his second great sermon, Peter said the same thing in slightly different words: "Repent, and be converted, that your sins may be blotted out…" That the Apostle Peter continued to preach repentance is clear from a dozen citations of the word in the Acts.

And did the Apostle Paul preach that same message? It is recorded that he was converted on the road to Damascus and began to preach, though the content of his message was not immediately recorded. But many years afterwards the Apostle himself declared what he had preached from the beginning: "I was not disobedient to the heavenly vision, but declared first to those at Damascus, then at Jerusalem, and throughout all the country of Judea, and also to the Gentiles, that they should repent, and turn to God, and perform deeds worthy of their repentance." The clear implication of the context is that he received a commission to preach repentance just as much as did the disciples in earlier times. And from other references in the Acts it is clear that he preached repentance to Jews and Gentiles.

Not only does the average Christian seem unaware of the first word of the good news, but he apparently does not know at all what the word means. To the average man, the word *repent* means "to feel sorry." Show him an item from the newspaper that a murderer has shown no repentance whatsoever for his evil deed, and he will explain that the fellow is not a bit sorry for what he has done.

The Greek scholar, Richard Trench, Archbishop of Dublin, defined the word *repentance* clearly as "that mighty change in mind, heart, and life, wrought by the Spirit of God." The word repentance, as used by modern Christians, does not signify a mighty change of mind, heart and life, but rather an emotional, sentimental experience better described by *regret* or *remorse*, for which an entirely different word is used in the Greek of the New Testament. The essential sense of the word repent is to change.

The Greek word *metanoia is* composed of two parts, *meta* meaning change, and *noia* meaning mind, hence *a revolution of thought*. But the meaning does not end there. It has a moral as well as an intellectual impact that is best summed up by the declaration of the Apostle Paul that he was commissioned to urge both Jews and Gentiles to revolutionize their thinking, and to turn to God and perform deeds worthy of their change of heart. Repentance may affect thinking, behaving, and feeling, as it was applied by Christ to Nicodemus, to the woman dragged by Pharisees before our Lord, or to the rich young ruler in early days; or as it now could be applied to a Buddhist priest, to an alcoholic, or to a lover of money on Wall Street. It clearly involved a thorough revolution of intellect, will and emotion.

How then did the meaning of repentance shift from *a mighty change of heart* to a lesser sense of regret? It is because of the use of the Latin word *repentance* which was derived from *paenitentia*, or a sense of pain or suffering, hence the grief for an act which might demand satisfaction, or the sorrow looking back upon something amiss. Unfortunately, the word *repent* is also used in the English Bible for a Greek verb properly translated "regret." In the Prayer Book, the words *repentance* and *penitence* are used interchangeably, causing endless confusion to this day.

Some mistaken people voice the strange notion that the Apostle Peter preached a message of repentance to the Jews, while the Apostle Paul preached "only believe" to Gentiles, and that when the Apostle Peter first preached to the household of Cornelius he did not use the particular word *repent.* A cursory reading of the story suggests that this was so. Cornelius, a captain of the Italian regiment, was "a devout man who feared God with all his household, gave alms liberally to the people, and prayed constantly to God." He obviously was a God-fearer rather than a convert to Judaism. The account of Peter's ministry and the whole company's conversion contains no reference to repentance in word or deed. But the next chapter, which recounts how the Apostle explained to the church at Jerusalem his odd conduct in disregarding the rules of segregation, concludes that they glorified God, saying: "Then to the Gentiles also God has granted repentance unto life." Whatever Cornelius did, the Holy Spirit designated it "repentance." But wherein did Cornelius change, if change is the proper translation? Did he cease to be devout? Did he cease to fear God? Did he stop giving alms? Did he quit praying constantly? No! Wherein did he change? Up until he heard the message of Peter he was struggling to obtain salvation by his good works; but after the message, he put his trust in the finished work of Christ. That was a change of thinking indeed.

The word *repentance* or *repent is* used in the writings of Paul to the Romans, the Corinthians, and Timothy, and by the writer to the Hebrews as well as by the Apostle Peter. It even occurs ten times in the Revelation of John. In all of the New Testament it appears more than fifty times. Hebrews lists it as an elementary doctrine of Christ, a foundation stone. How serious then is the condition of a professing church when repentance is missing from elementary evangelism or church growth?

The three parables of our Lord in the fifteenth chapter of Luke's Gospel are often called "the Gospel Parables," or the parables of evangelism. They are the well-known stories of the lost sheep, the lost coin and the lost son. The ending of each has a peculiar significance. The shepherd called together his friends and neighbours and invited them to rejoice with him that he had found his sheep that was lost. That is the end of the story, but the Lord quickly added: "Just so, I tell you, there will be more joy in heaven over one sinner who repents than over ninety-nine righteous persons who need no repentance." Why such an explanation? If he had not explained, someone would have insisted that as the sheep did not repent, there was not need of repentance for salvation. The woman who lost a coin called together her friends likewise that they might rejoice with her that she had found her lost coin. That is the end of the story, but the Lord quickly added: "Just so, I tell you, there is joy before the angels of God over one sinner who repents." Why the explanation? Some theologian might have insisted that as a coin is incapable of repenting, repentance is not needed for salvation. But the story of the lost son has no such explanation attached to its ending. Why? Repentance is clearly stated in the narrative when the prodigal son told his father: "Father, I have sinned against heaven, and in your sight; I am no longer worthy to be called your son." The addition, or lack of addition, of repentance is very significant, underlining its importance.

Sad to say, repentance is a missing note in much modern evangelism. The appeal is not for repentance but rather for enlistment. Thirty years ago, the notorious gangster, Mr. Mickey Cohen, attended a meeting in Beverly Hills which was addressed by Billy Graham and chaired by the writer. He expressed some interest in the message so several of us talked with him, including Dr. Graham. He made no commitment until some time later when another friend urged him, using Revelation 3:20 as a warrant, to invite Jesus Christ into his life. This he professed to do, but his life subsequently gave no evidence of repentance, "that mighty change of mind, heart and life." He rebuked our friend, telling him: "You did not tell me that I would have to give up my work," meaning his rackets; "You did not tell me that I would have to give up my friends," meaning his gangster associates. He had heard that so-and-so was a Christian football player, so-and-so a Christian cowboy, so-and-so a Christian actress, so-and-so a Christian senator, and he really thought that he could be a Christian gangster. Alas, there was not evidence of repentance. Many have sadly forgotten that the only evidence of the new birth is the new life. The real problem is that some evangelists, like some converts, have failed to recognize that the fault lies in the defective message.

Defective evangelism has become a national scandal. While evangelistic enterprises are claiming untold numbers of converts, a national poll announcing that multi-millions claim to be "born-again," yet a national newspaper notes that the "so-called evangelical awakening" seems to have had no effect upon the morals of the nation, while murder, robbery, rape, prostitution, pornography and the other social evils are abounding. The fault must lie in the message, for in the great awakenings of the past, sinners were urged to repent and believe the gospel.

Many earnest Christians have raised the question: "Does not the Scripture teach that 'only believe' is all that is necessary? Did not the Apostle Paul tell the Philippian jailer simply: 'Believe on the Lord Jesus Christ and you will be saved?'" Quite so. But to whom were these words addressed? To a jailer who had cruelly beaten his helpless prisoners, but who was now so frightened that he had fallen on his knees to cry: "What must I do to be saved?" Had he repented? Of course. He had changed his attitude, so the Apostle reassured him that now all that he needed to do was to put his trust in the Lord Jesus Christ to be saved.

After all, there is no question that it was the Lord Jesus Christ himself who said: "Repent and believe the gospel." Some immediately react by supposing that this contradicts the "only believe" of the Christian message. Does "repent and believe the gospel" imply that the sinner must do two things to be saved, and not one only? The exhortation is really only one requirement. The instruction: "Leave Los Angeles and go to London" may sound like two separate but related requests, but it really is only one, for it is quite impossible to go to London without leaving Los Angeles. It is likewise quite impossible to believe truly without really repenting. The difference between true faith and what the Scripture calls false faith is simple: it is the lack of true repentance. Without a doubt, many who seek to win sinners to the Saviour without specifying repentance in their gospel presentation nevertheless hope that true repentance, that mighty change of mind, heart and life, will ensue, rejoicing when it happens. But their disappointment when it does not happen should compel them to reword their message so that there can be no misunderstanding whatever.

Strange to relate, many Christians do not realize that the word *repent* is also a word for the continuing Christian life. Not only is the word repent the entrance to new life in Christ, but it is an exhortation of Christ himself for the believer in continuing in the Christian life. But that is a topic for consideration elsewhere. It is sufficient to emphasize in the present context that not only is evangelism defective without the opening word *repentance*, but that many baffled believers may be suffering defeat because of the primary neglect of repentance when they first professed to believe in the Lord Jesus Christ.

1   Keith and Gladys Hunt, *For Christ and the University: The Story of InterVarsity Christian Fellowship of the U.S.A./1940–1990* (Downers Grove, Illinois: InterVarsity Press, 1991), 59–60.

2   David M. Howard, *Student Power in World Evangelism* (Downers Grove, Illinois: InterVarsity Press, 1971), 99–101.

3   Hunt, *For Christ and the University*, 121–130.

4   J.E. Orr, *The Re-Study of Revival and Revivalism* (Pasadena, California: School of World Mission, 1981), 49.

5   J.E. Orr, *Campus Aflame* (Glendale, California: Gospel Light Publications, 1971), 145.

6   A.J. Appasamy, *Write the Vision* (Port Washington, Pennsylvania: Christian Literature Crusade, 1964), 149–150.

7   The message by Orr provided at the conclusion of this chapter entitled *The First Word of the Gospel* was originally composed during this era of collegiate revivals.

8   Appasamy, *Write the Vision*, 150–151.

9   W.W. Willard, *Fire on the Prairie* (Wheaton College, Illinois: Van Kampen Press, 1950), 188.

10   *Time*, February 20, 1950.

11   H.C. James and Paul Rader, *Halls Aflame* (Wilmore, Kentucky: The Dept. of Evangelism, Asbury Theological Seminary, 1966), 9.

12   J.E. Orr, *Good News in Bad Times* (Grand Rapids, Michigan: Zondervan, 1953), 64–85.

13   Joseph T. Bayly, "Editorial," *HIS Magazine* 16, no.4 (January 1956), 2, citing Stanley Rowland in *The New York Times*, (October 22 and October 24, 1955).

14   *HIS Magazine* 11, no.4 (January 1951), 29; 11, no.5 (February 1951), 23; 11, no.6 (March 1951), 35; 11, no.7 (April 1951), 12; 11, no.8 (May 1951), 26–28.

15   Hunt, *For Christ and the University*, 392–412. The InterVarsity website tells of current statistics: http://www.ivcf.org/aboutiv/history.html.

16   William R. Bright, *Come Help Change the World* (San Bernardino: Here's Life Publishers, Inc., 1985), passim; information taken from the Campus Crusade for Christ website: http://home.ccci.org.

17   Betty Lee Skinner, *Daws* (Colorado Springs, Colorado: Navpress, 1994), 272; Lorne Sanny, past president of Navigators, telephone interview by author, *c.*1994; Steve Rugg, Director of Operations for Collegiate Ministry of the Navigators, telephone interview by author, October 30, 2001.

18   Ralph D. Winter, *The Twenty-Five Unbelievable Years* (South Pasadena, California: William Carey Library, 1971), 56–57. Statistics for Inter-Varsity come from their website: www.ivcf.org/aboutiv/history.html.

19   Howard, *Student Power in World Evangelism*, 104.

20   John Nelson and Janet Rohler, "Asbury Revival Blazes Cross-Country Trail,"

Christianity Today 14, no.12 (March 13, 1970), 46–50.

21 Robert E. Coleman, ed., *One Divine Moment* (Old Tappen, New Jersey: Fleming H. Revell Co., 1970), 55.

22 "College Revival 1995—Spiritual Revival on College Campuses" (Chicago: Moody Broadcasting Network Cassette Ministry, 1995), Tape 1.

23 "College Revival 1995—Spiritual Revival on College Campuses," Tape 1.

24 "College Revival 1995—Spiritual Revival on College Campuses," Tape 3.

25 Stephen B. Kellough, Memorandum on Spiritual Awakening on Campus, Thursday, March 23, 1995, to the Wheaton College faculty and staff.

26 "College Revival 1995—Spiritual Revival on College Campuses," Tape 1.

27 "College Revival 1995—Spiritual Revival on College Campuses," Tape 2.

28 *The Brethren Evangelist* 117, no. 6 (June 1995), 10.

29 Appasamy, *Write the Vision*, 149.

30 This sermon has been provided in its complete from, and can be found in the book by J. Edwin Orr, *My All His All*, ed. Richard Owen Roberts (Wheaton, Illinois: International Awakening Press, 1989), 1–9 and is used with permission of Richard Owen Roberts. Scripture quotations approximate the KJV but were quoted from the author's memory.

6

Principles and patterns of campus revivals

Background

You have just walked through nearly two centuries of the history of revival on American campuses. Is another campus revival imminent? When will God walk again on campus? To paraphrase the disciples' query posed to the risen Christ in Acts 1:6: "Lord, when will you come and revive our campus, as you have done in times past?" As he replied to that generation, so he would say to us: "It is not for you to know the times or dates the Father has set by his own authority." The exact timing of the next awakening is known only to God the Father; it is a date "the Father has set by his own authority."

However, it is my conviction that the Christian community can notably benefit from understanding the principles and patterns common to seasons of collegiate awakenings. This final chapter will seek to provide such an overview. It is likewise my conviction that although the integration and practice of these concepts will not *cause* another revival—the giver of such is God alone—these collective principles and patterns can assist believers in shaping a context of ministry where God is honoured more purely, Christ obeyed more readily and the Holy Spirit less likely to be grieved.

Principles and patterns

1. Prompted prayer

When God desires to bring about an awakening, he calls his people to prayer. Such was the case at Brown University early in the nineteenth century when the Spirit, prior to visiting that particular campus with an awakening, prompted three students to form a "College Praying Society."[1] Coinciding with various awakenings at Yale, Williams, Harvard and Middlebury Colleges, Christ likewise called groups of students to host concerts of prayer.[2] Perhaps the most notable nineteenth-century illustration is in what some have called the "Prayer Meeting Revival" of 1858–1859, when vast numbers from both the collegiate and non-collegiate communities were led to entreat for yet another outpouring of divine grace.

There is a similar pattern in twentieth-century awakenings. When the Spirit of revival descended on Eastern Nazarene College in 1930, for example, classrooms were turned into prayer rooms. Mealtimes found the dining hall of this institution nearly empty, as students devoted themselves instead to prayer and fasting.[3] During the same decade, students at Wheaton had a similar experience following a routine chapel service. Many of the students were "on their faces" in repentant prayer.[4] And it was a small meeting, where four gathered in Billy Graham's Minnesota office to pray, that many credit as being a central component of the mid-century college awakenings.[5]

Although the particular timing of any revival is known and governed by God alone, in his marvellous kindness he calls the Christian community to freely, deliberately and with persistence express their yearnings for future outpourings. When earnest believers are compelled by the Spirit to steadfast intercession, Christians should take heart, because history has demonstrated the fact that when God desires to bring about an awakening, he moves his people to prayer. Moreover, such prayer is evidence of what American historian Richard Lovelace has called "radical dependence on the Spirit,"[6] a recognition that the Holy Spirit is the true agent of renewal and revival.

2. Conviction and confession

The extraordinary conviction of sin accompanied by genuine confession is also commonplace during seasons of collegiate revival.

Recall the story of the awakening at Amherst in 1858 when such a powerful conviction of sin gripped the students that "the entire collegiate community was brought under its influence." Confession of sin followed, and nearly all of the students at Amherst during that awakening were converted![7] L.D. Wishard, recounting his days at Princeton in the latter part of the nineteenth century, remembers a time of penetrating conviction when "men by the dozen and by the score began to ask the question of the Philippian jailer."[8]

And was not the 1904–1905 revival characterized by such "an intense sensation of the presence of God" that it led to subsequent conviction and confession of sin?[9] The various campuses across the States that were graced by the general collegiate visitation of 1936 commonly experienced "deep conviction, a thorough confession" followed by "immediate restitution."[10] So powerful was the presence of the Spirit at Bethel Chapel in 1949 that

> there was much prayer in the dormitories, followed by intense conviction of sin among the students in chapel and in classroom. Conviction was relieved only by outright confession, restitution, restoration or conversion to God.[11]

Wheaton College knew a similar awakening early in 1950, when "all night long, all the next day, all through the following night, and half of the following day, students poured out confessions of past sins and rededicated themselves to God."[12] Students present at the various schools impacted by the 1970 Asbury revival, along with numerous others who experienced the Spring 1995 collegiate visitation, share similar stories of strong conviction, genuine confession and the reality of sweet forgiveness.[13]

3. Biblical priorities

One of the great tragedies of higher education over the past two centuries has been the movement of many academic institutions away from their Christian moorings, a clear commitment to the

Scriptures and related biblical priorities. The history of many student Christian movements followed a similar lamentable pattern, with the progressive deterioration of the YMCA as a potent evangelical association furnishing perhaps the best illustration. For over a half century this organization was used mightily by God to advance the kingdom in academic and non-academic settings alike. It was not until the YMCA made the unfortunate choice early in the twentieth century to focus less on biblical priorities, such as evangelism, missions, and strong scriptural teaching, that a 25,000 member decline was experienced among their Bible study groups.[14] Not surprisingly, revival visitations to YMCA chapters likewise dwindled.

By contrast, the sermons of Timothy Dwight, C.H. Spurgeon, D. Martyn Lloyd-Jones, and J. Edwin Orr reveal dynamic, Word-centred preaching that is at the heart of all true biblical revival. Do you hear messages like these within your student fellowship group? Many would agree that such teaching is uncommon in this day and age. It was likewise scarce during those campus revivals that were predominantly experienced-based. Dwight, Spurgeon, Lloyd-Jones and Orr have all departed this earth, but do we not need some within *this* generation who will pick up the torch of the Word and, with a similar disciplined commitment, teach the deep and abiding truths of Scripture? May Christian campus leadership be vigilant to maintain sound Word-centred ministries that place due emphasis on vital Christian doctrine and related biblical priorities and so help herald the way for genuine revival.

4. Student directed

Collegiate ministry is strongest when students are empowered to be the fundamental leaders of their respective groups or ministries. This is not to suggest that Christian faculty, administrators, pastors, evangelists, chaplains or other related staff are not an integral part of a vital and growing student movement. Quite the contrary. Mature non-student leaders such as Dwight L. Moody, Luther D. Wishard and J. Edwin Orr, to name only three, were indeed integral to the collegiate awakenings of their day. The roles they played among student leadership, however, were primarily to assist in the advancement of a strong Word-centred ministry through teaching, evangelizing, encouraging and equipping for service, rather than to domineer or inappropriately control.

In 1815, for example, it was the students who initiated and led concerts of prayer at Brown, Yale and Middlebury.[15] Williams College, about a decade earlier, boarded a freshman by the name of Samuel J. Mills who, along with various peers, was burdened by God to organize the first foreign missionary society in America.[16] One might recall the story of the three students praying at Hampden-Sydney College, who, when confronted with insults from their unbelieving peers, chose instead to heed the encouragement of the college president and continue their discipline of prayer. Their small group was soon joined by half of the student body, and finally by the presence of the Spirit of the revival, who caused an awakening that swept campus and community alike.[17] In the same period of time, a student who boldly and openly opposed the reading of questionable literature in the classroom was instrumental in kindling revival fires at Denison College, in Marietta, Ohio.[18]

5. Ministry and missions

During seasons of revival, the call to vocational ministry both at home and abroad becomes irresistible. This was certainly the case at Yale College when, as a result of the 1802 awakening, one out of every six students was led by the Spirit to pursue a call to vocational ministry.[19] At Princeton, during the same era, it was nearly half of those converted who pledged their lives to such service.[20] Five decades later, Princeton rejoiced in another awakening that resulted in a documented one hundred professions of faith, with a full fifty of that number subsequently called to ministry.[21] Bowdoin College boasted that a quarter of its 1850 graduating class, a majority of whom had been impacted by revival, became "ministers of the gospel."[22] The twentieth century awakenings recount similar stories.

Student mission movements sparked by revival fires were likewise numerous. From the historic 1806 Haystack prayer meeting at Williams College to the turn-of-the-century Student Volunteer Movements, untold multitudes of young collegiate missionaries have been both challenged and called to foreign service. In the year immediately following the 1904–1905 Revival, for example, a record 3,500 students sailed to distant and unreached people groups around the globe to spread the good news of the gospel.[23] After World War II numerous veterans, burdened by the spiritual need of many of the nations they saw during their military service, returned to foreign soil as ambassadors for Christ. Many of the missions conferences and para-church ministries that were either initiated or strengthened during the 1950s campus awakenings still continue today, sending out numbers of students annually to work for Christ.

6. Cross-denominational focus

Although there are basic orthodox doctrinal parameters to which each believer must ascribe, the collegiate student groups birthed or sustained by the Spirit in revival are traditionally inter-denominational in both philosophy and composition. Historical illustrations of this pattern are legion. When J.R. Mott in the late nineteenth century established the World Student Christian Federation he suggested that:

> The very genius and purpose of a Christian Association, like that of its Lord, should be to unite all real disciples of Jesus Christ without reference to their denominational affiliations, wealth, fraternity connections, athletic reputation, intellectual standing, or life-plans. There are problems in connection with the moral and religious life of nearly every institution which cannot be solved unless all right-thinking Christian men sink their minor differences and unite for this definite purpose.[24]

The YMCA was likewise inter-denominational in both philosophy and practice. "Christ for the students of the world, and the students of the world for Christ" was the heartbeat of the first YMCA student secretary, Luther Wishard, who saw this predominately collegiate organization grow to 22,241 members representing various denominational backgrounds only fourteen short years after his appointment to this post.[25] When revival visited Asbury College in the spring of 1970, waves of Asbury students poured out from the small Kentucky town to no less than 130 colleges, seminaries, and Bible schools of diverse denominational backgrounds to tell of God's wonder, power and grace.[26] The student leadership involved in the spring 1995 collegiate awakening followed a similar pattern. In the campus awakenings we have surveyed the primary emphasis has been given not to denominational distinctives, important though these might be in their own right, but to Christ, Scripture, prayer, outreach and missions. May these same priorities be found in our collegiate fellowships today!

For reflection

1. Imagine that an outsider was requested to spend several months at your college or university to evaluate the school based upon the criteria outlined in this final chapter. How do you believe they would respond to the following question? On a scale of 1 to 5 (one being poor, five being outstanding), rate the Christian students and/or fellowship group(s) at your school in the following categories:

   a) Practicing disciplined, sustained prayer

   b) Responsive to conviction and earnest in confession

   c) Studying, practicing and, when applicable, teaching the Scriptures

   d) Strong student involvement within meetings and related ministries

   e) Service through short-term and vocational missions/ministry

   f) Inter-denominational in focus

2. Imagine again that the president of the student fellowship on your campus heard of the findings of this evaluation and sent you or your small group the following written request: Please assemble several recommendations for our student fellowship based upon your own personal observations and information gathered from the evaluation. The following guidelines would be important for you to consider as you write:

   a) Are these recommendations ones that you are personally willing to follow?

   b) Specifically, how would you advise that one might initiate your suggestions?

3. No more imagination. It is today, and your journey through revival history is coming to a close—or is it? That is a question you will need to decide. Ponder the following challenges. There are two, and I need to caution you, because if you say "yes" to either one, your own walk with God may never be the same!

   a) Are you willing to bring the recommendations you outlined in Question 2 to Christians at your school, students or others in leader ship positions, who may be able to dialogue with you concerning their implementation? If "yes," make specific plans.

   b) Are you willing to take this journey again? Is the Spirit prompting your heart to enlist the interest of a small group to journey again through these pages? Consider your own personal experience over the past weeks, and then ask God if he desires to use you in bringing that experience to others.

Ponder these challenges, and before you close the book I would exhort you to make a specific application.

1   Clarence P. Shedd, *Two Centuries of Student Christian Movements* (New York: Association Press, 1934), 41.

2   Shedd, *Two Centuries*, 82.

3   J. Cameron, *Eastern Nazarene College* (Kansas City, Missouri: Nazarene Publishing House, 1968), 201.

4   J.E. Orr, *This is the Victory* (Grand Rapids: Zondervan Publishing House, 1936), 37.

5   A.J. Appasamy, *Write the Vision* (Port Washington, Pennsylvania: Christian Literature Crusade, 1964), 149–150.

6   "Pneumatological Issues in American Presbyterianism," *Greek Orthodox Theological Review*, 31 (1986), 345–346.

7   *The Oberlin Evangelist* (12 May, 1858).

8   L.D. Wishard, "The Beginning of the Students' Era in Christian History" (Unpublished manuscript, 1917, Y.M.C.A. Historical Library), 56.

9   Orr, *The Flaming Tongue* (Chicago: Moody Press, 1973), 72.

10 Appasamy, *Write the Vision*, 148.

11 Appasamy, *Write the Vision*, 150–151.

12 *Time*, February 20, 1950

13 As a rule, the Scriptures teach that *private* sin is to be confessed before God, to the offended party (Matthew 18:15), or in the presence of mature Christian leaders (James 5:14–16). There are no general biblical exhortations for the confession of private sin before a corporate body of believers (except in extreme cases as noted in Matthew 18:17). A helpful guideline to follow, therefore, during a time of Spirit-led public confession is to permit only the sins that have offended the entire body of believers present (false slanderous statements spoken against a Christian community, for example) to be confessed publicly whereas those sins that are private in nature (sexual immorality, ethical compromises, etc.) confessed in the presence of several mature Christian leaders or directly to the offended party.

14 C. Howard Hopkins, *History of the Y.M.C.A. in North America* (New York:

Association Press, 1951), 644–645.

[15] Shedd, 82.

[16] T.C. Richards, *The Life of Samuel J. Mills* (Boston, New York: The Pilgrim Press, 1906), 26–35.

[17] C.L. Thompson, *Times of Refreshing, A History of American Revivals from 1740–1877* (Chicago: J.S. Goodman, 1877), 79.

[18] F. Rudolph, *The American College and University* (New York: Knopf, 1962), 81.

[19] "Religion in Colleges," *The Princeton Review* 31, No.1 (January, 1859), 42.

[20] Benjamin Rice Lacy, Jr., *Revivals in the Midst of the Years* (1943 ed.; repr. Hopewell, Virginia: Royal Publishers, Inc.,1968), 93.

[21] J. Edwin Orr, *The Event of the Century*, ed. Richard Owen Roberts, (Wheaton, Illinois: International Awakening Press, 1989), 182.

[22] "Religion in Colleges," 41–42.

[23] *Missionary Review of the World* (May 1906), 370.

[24] Basil Mathews, *John R. Mott, World Citizen* (New York/London: Harper and Brothers, 1934), 103.

[25] C. Howard Hopkins, *History of the Y.M.C.A.* 271, 282–283.

[26] Robert E. Coleman, ed., *One Divine Moment* (Old Tappen, New Jersey: Fleming H. Revell Co., 1970), 55.

Appendix

J. Edwin Orr (1912–1987): Historian of Revival[1]

by Michael A.G. Haykin

Does God call men and women to be historians? If this question sounds odd to our ears, possibly it's because we do not take seriously enough the biblical view of vocation. Without a doubt, if we could have asked this question of Luke, the historian of the early Church, his answer would have been an unequivocal yes. And Luke's affirmation would be echoed by a number throughout the past two thousand years whom the Lord has used to record and reflect on the history of his church. One of this number was J. Edwin Orr, student and historian of revival and spiritual awakenings, who died on April 22 of this year [1987].

Born in 1912 in Northern Ireland of American-Irish parentage, Orr was led to Christ by a godly mother when he was nine years old. As Orr later described his conversion:

> [My mother] held the theory that a child's heart takes impressions like wax but keeps them like marble: so she believed that no child was really too young to trust the Lord for salvation.[2]

Eight years later, when he was seventeen, Orr was baptized in Great Victoria Street Baptist Church in Belfast and soon found himself contemplating Christian ministry. Of great significance was the formation at this time of a "Revival Fellowship" with some friends. Its goal was, in Orr's words, "to pray for spiritual awakening around the world."[3]

Orr's early ministry in the 1930s and the early 1940s was as an itinerant revivalist "travelling from Land's End to John O'Groats in the British Isles, and from Gibraltar to Moscow, from Oslo to Jerusalem" as well as covering the United States and what were then the British Dominions—New Zealand, Australia, South Africa and Canada.[4]

On his tour of Canada in 1935, for instance, Orr went from the Atlantic to Pacific, sharing his vision for revival in such diverse places as the Feller Institute of the Grande Ligne Mission in Quebec, People's Church in Toronto, Delta Tabernacle in Hamilton, St James Anglican Church in Saskatoon, Prairie Bible Institute at Three Hills and Ruth Morton Baptist Church in Vancouver. His observations on the spiritual state of Canada are still strikingly relevant. He found many Canadians absorbed with materialism, and within the churches a corresponding dearth of prayer meetings and evangelism. He also noted "that there has never been a Canadian national revival" and urged Canadian Christians pray for such a move of the Spirit.[5]

But it was during the war years that Orr entered upon what would probably be his most fruitful area of ministry, namely, the charting of the ways that God has moved in revival in the past. Orr took a Th.D. at Northern Baptist Seminary in Chicago and then a D.Phil. at Oxford. The subject of his theses at both these institutions was the 1859 Revival, studies which later found their way into print as *The Second Evangelical Awakening in America* and *The Second Evangelical Awakening in Britain*. These studies, however, were interrupted by three years or so of military service as a chaplain with the American Air Force in the Pacific. But this interruption only served to provide a context in which God gave Orr assurance of his calling as an historian, a historian of revival. Orr described this assurance which he received in the following way in the Introduction to *The Second Evangelical Awakening*:

In 1945, the author was pacing along a beach-head in the Pacific following a heavy air-raid, wondering whether or not he would survive the war. That night came a strange assurance from God that his life would be spared for a twofold purpose—to become a historian of the great Nineteenth Century Awakening, hitherto unchronicled, and to be an eyewitness of the beginnings of the Twentieth Century Awakening, long desired.[6]

From this point on, Orr devoted much of his time to research and write books on revival such as *The Light of the Nations: Evangelical Renewal and Advance in the Nineteenth Century* (1965), *The Flaming Tongue: The Impact of Twentieth Century Revivals* (1973) and *The Eager Feet: Evangelical Awakenings, 1790–1830* (1975). Although Orr regarded many of these books as pioneer studies, his research did lead him to a number of definite convictions about revival, two of which especially bear mentioning.

The first relates to the role that prayer plays in revival and spiritual wakening. For instance, in recounting the revival that spread out from Great Britain and the United States in the early nineteenth century, Orr stated:

> The Concert of Prayer for revival in the 1780s in Great Britain and in the 1790s in the United States, and the renewed Concert of Prayer in both countries in 1815 and in several European realms besides, was clearly demonstrated to be the prime factor in motivation and equipping Christians for service in a worldwide movement which totally eclipsed the military might of the nations at the Battle of Waterloo [in 1815].[7]

In fact, as Orr details, it was John Sutcliff of Olney (1754–1814) who, influenced especially by Jonathan Edwards, the American pastor and theologian of revival, urged his fellow Baptist ministers to pray for an outpouring of the Holy Spirit.[8] From such humble beginnings came a worldwide awakening. This vital role of prayer, especially corporate prayer, in revival is something we need to ponder afresh.

The second conviction with regard to revival which Orr came to stress in his later writings was that revival is a sovereign work of the Holy Spirit. In answer to the question about the ultimate origins of revival, Orr stated:

> Is revival a work of God, as Jonathan Edwards insisted, or a work of man, as C.G. Finney proposed? The biblical answer is clear: 'Will you not revive us again?' cried the Psalmist; 'Revive your work, O Lord!' requested the prophet; and both petitions were addressed to God. Nowhere in Scripture is any suggestion of plan or program for self-revival.[9]

By this answer Orr in no way wished to deny that men had a part to play in revival. Prayer, preaching, calling for repentance and conversion—all of these men had to do. But through his study of revival Orr had come to recognize that ultimately "neither denomination nor organisation, nor pastor nor evangelist, can organise an outpouring of the Holy Spirit."[10] The final verse of Orr's well-known hymn "Cleanse Me" well sums up this conviction and forms a fitting conclusion, and challenge, to this brief appreciation of the work of J. Edwin Orr, historian of revival:

> *O Holy Ghost,*
> *Revival comes from Thee;*
> *Send a revival,*
> *Start the work in me.*

[1]   This Appendix first appeared as "J. Edwin Orr (1912–1987): Historian of Revival," *The Banner of Truth*, 294 (March 1988), 18–20, 26. It is reprinted here with slight modifications and with the permission of The Banner of Truth Trust.
[2]   *Full Surrender* (London/Edinburgh: 1951), 117. In this book Orr deals with such topics as the nature of sanctification and the fullness of the Spirit. His perspective on these subjects is clearly that favoured by the exponents of what J.I. Packer has called the "Keswick teaching" (*Keep In Step With the Spirit* [Old

Tappan, New Jersey: Fleming H. Revell Co., 1984], 145–163).

3 *Full Surrender*, 119.

4 *Full Surrender*, 123–124.

5 *Times of Refreshing* (London/Edinburgh: Marshall, Morgan & Scott, Ltd., 1936), 112–115.

6 *The Second Evangelical Awakening. An account of the Second Worldwide Evangelical Revival beginning in the Mid-Nineteenth Century* (Abridged ed.; London/Edinburgh: Marshall, Morgan & Scott, 1955), ix.

7 *The Eager Feet. Evangelical Awakenings, 1790–1830* (Chicago: 1975), 95.

8 On Sutcliff and what was called "The Prayer Call of 1784", see Michael A.G. Haykin, *One heart and one soul: John Sutcliff of Olney, his friends, and his times* (Darlington, Co. Durham: Evangelical Press, 1994).

9 *Eager Feet*, 14–16, 191, 199.

10 *The Outpouring of the Spirit in Revival and Awakening and its Issue in Church Growth* ([Pasadena, California]: 198), 4. This essay summarizes much of Orr's research into revivals of the past.

Select bibliography

Appasamy, A.J. *Write the Vision*. Port Washington, Pennsylvania: Christian Literature Crusade, 1964.

Beardsley, F.G. *A History of American Revivals*. New York: American Tract Society, 1904.

Beecher, Charles, ed. *Autobiography, Correspondence, Etc. of Lyman Beecher, D.D.* New York: Harper & Brothers, 1864.

Bradley, Joshua. *Accounts of Religious Revivals in Many Parts of the United States from 1815–1818*. Wheaton, Illinois: Richard Owen, Publishers, 1980.

Cameron, J. *Eastern Nazarene College*. Kansas City, Missouri: Nazarene Publishing House, 1968.

Chessman, G. W. *Denison: The Story of an Ohio College*. Grandville, Ohio: Denison University, 1957.

Coleman, Robert E., ed. *One Divine Moment*. Old Tappan, New Jersey: Fleming H. Revell Co., 1970

Conant, W.C. *Narrative of Remarkable Conversion*. New York: Derby and Jackson, 1858.

Coulter, E.M. *College Life in the Old South*. Athens, Georgia: University of Georgia Press, 1951.

Dwight, Timothy. *Theology Explained and Defended in a Series of Sermons; With a Memoir of the Author's Life*. New York: Harper, 1846. 5 vols.

Gleason, Michael F. *Building on Living Stones: New Testament Patterns and Principles of Renewal.* Grand Rapids, Michigan: Kregel Publications, 1996.

Godbold, A. *The Church College of the Old South.* Durham: Duke University Press, 1944.

Hoffman, Fred W. *Revival Times in America.* Boston: W.A. Wilde Co., 1956.

Hopkins, C. Howard. *History of the Y.M.C.A. in North America.* New York: Association Press, 1951.

Howard, David M. *Student Power in World Evangelism.* Downers Grove, Illinois: InterVarsity Press, 1971.

Hunt, Keith and Gladys Hunt. *For Christ and the University: The Story of InterVarsity Christian Fellowship of the U.S.A./1940–1990.* Downers Grove, Illinois: InterVarsity Press, 1991.

James, H.C. and Paul Rader. *Halls Aflame.* Wilmore, Kentucky: The Dept. of Evangelism, Asbury Theological Seminary, 1966.

Lacy, Jr., Benjamin Rice. *Revivals in the Midst of the Years.* 1943. Reprint, Hopewell, Virginia: Royal Publishers, Inc., 1968.

Larson, Mel. *Young Man on Fire: The Story of Torrey Johnson and Youth For Christ.* Chicago: Youth Publications, 1945.

Latourette, K.S. *Beyond the Ranges.* Grand Rapids, Michigan: Wm. B. Eerdmans, 1967.

Lewis, Elvet G., G. Campbell Morgan and I.V. Neprash. *Glory Filled the Land. A Trilogy on the Welsh Revival, 1904–1905.* Ed. Richard Owen Roberts. Wheaton, Illinois: International Awakening Press, 1989.

Lloyd-Jones, Martyn. *Revival.* Wheaton, Illinois: Crossway Books, 1987.

Mathews, Basil. *John R. Mott, World Citizen.* New York/London: Harper & Brothers, 1934.

Morison, S.E. *Three Centuries of Harvard, 1636–1936*. Cambridge, Massachusetts: Harvard University Press, 1936.

Noble, W.F.P. *A Century of Gospel Work*. Philadelphia, Pennsylvania: H.C. Watts & Co/San Francisco: Al Bancroft & Co., 1876.

Orr, J. Edwin. *Campus Aflame*. Glendale, California: Regal Books, 1971.

Orr, J. Edwin. *The Event of the Century*. Ed. Richard Owen Roberts. Wheaton, Illinois: International Awakening Press, 1989.

Orr, J. Edwin. *The Flaming Tongue*. Chicago: Moody Press, 1973.

Orr, J. Edwin. *Good News in Bad Times*. Grand Rapids, Michigan: Zondervan, 1953.

Orr, J. Edwin. *The Light of the Nations*. Grand Rapids, Michigan: Wm. B. Eerdmans Publishing Co., 1965.

Orr, J. Edwin. *My All His All*. Ed. Richard Owen Roberts. Wheaton, Illinois: International Awakening Press, 1989.

Orr, J. Edwin. *The Re-Study of Revival and Revivalism*. Pasadena, California: The School of World Missions, 1981.

Orr, J. Edwin. *This is the Victory*. Grand Rapids, Michigan: Zondervan Publishing House: 1936.

Richards, T.C. *Samuel J. Mills*. Boston/New York: The Pilgrim Press, 1906.

Roberts, Richard Owen. *Whitefield In Print*. Wheaton, Illinois: Richard Owen Roberts Publishers, 1988.

Rudolph, F. *Mark Hopkins and the Log: Williams College, 1836–1872*. New Haven: Yale University Press, 1956.

Rudolph, F. *The American College and University*. New York: Knopf, 1962.

Shedd, Clarence P. *Two Centuries of Student Christian Movements.* New York: Association Press, 1934.

Shedd, Clarence P. *The Church Follows Its Students.* New York: Yale University Press, 1938.

Skinner, Betty Lee. *Daws.* Colorado Springs, Colorado: Navpress, 1994.

Smith, S.A. *The American College Chaplaincy.* New York: Association Press, 1954.

Spurgeon, C.H. *Sermons on Revival.* Ed. Charles T. Cook. Grand Rapids, Michigan: Zondervan Publishing House, 1958.

Spurgeon, C.H. *Revival Year Sermons.* London: The Banner of Truth Trust, 1959.

Strickland, A.B. *The Great American Revival.* Cincinnati: Standard Press, 1934.

Sweet, William Warren, *The Story of Religion in America.* New York/London: Harper & Brothers, 1930 and 1939.

Thompson, C.L. *Times of Refreshing: A History of American Revivals from 1740–1877.* Chicago: J. S. Goodman, 1877.

Wertenbaker, T.J. *Princeton: 1746–1896.* Princeton, New Jersey: Princeton University Press, 1946.

Willard, W.W. *Fire on the Prairie.* Wheaton College, Illinois: Van Kampen Press, 1950.

Winter, Ralph D. *The Twenty-Five Unbelievable Years.* South Pasadena, California: William Carey Library, 1971.

Wishard, L.D. "The Beginning of the Students' Era in Christian History." Unpublished manuscript, 1917. Y.M.C.A. Historical Library.

Wright, H.B. *Two Centuries of Christian Activity at Yale.* New York: G.P. Putnam & Sons, 1901.

Heavenly fire

The life and ministry of William Grimshaw of Haworth

by Esther Bennett

Though little known today, William Grimshaw was a powerful force in the Evangelical Revival in the north of England in the eighteenth-century. Under his tireless ministry, hundreds in the town of Haworth and the surrounding vicinity came to know Christ. Esther Bennett writes an engaging overview of his life and ministry which will inspire and encourage today's readers in what God can do in the hearts of men and women through his word and the power of his Spirit.

ISBN 1-894400-08-9, 24 pages, 8" x 8", saddle-stitch, colour, softcover

Order online at www.joshuapress.com